Profoundly Superficial

Observations on a Net Zero Culture

Also by David Solway from New English Review Press:

Crossing the Jordan: On Judaism, Islam, and the West
(2023)

Profoundly Superficial

Observations on a Net Zero Culture

David Solway

Published by New English Review Press
a subsidiary of World Encounter Institute
PO Box 158397
Nashville, Tennessee 37215
&
27 Old Gloucester Street
London, England, WC1N 3AX

Cover art and design by Kendra Mallock

ISBN: 978-1-966833-04-8
Library of Congress Control Number: 2025943488

First Edition

NEW ENGLISH REVIEW PRESS
newenglishreview.org

This book is dedicated to President Donald Trump for his determination to purge the nation of incompetents, traitors, and the myriad clowns and dimwits on the political dole who promote pottery classes in Morocco, tourism in Lebanon, Sesame Street in Iraq, DEI in Serbia, and transgender comic books in Peru while pocketing the skim.

A wordy, watery age
That whispered to the sun's compassion, made
A convocation, nightly, of the sea-stars,
And on the cropping foot-ways of the moon
Lay grovelling.
— Wallace Stevens, *The Comedian as the Letter C*

They shed their sense of responsibility
Long ago, when they lost their votes, and the bribes; the mob
That used to grant power, high office, the legions, everything,
Curtails its desires, and reveals its anxiety for two things only,
Bread and circuses.
— Juvenal, *The Satires*, X

CONTENTS

INTRODUCTION

Those who will not reason, are bigots, those who cannot, are fools, and those who dare not, are slaves.
— George Gordon, Lord Byron, *The Two Foscari*

An abysmal place, Earth. Oh, don't get me wrong! A thousand years ago it had character — the Crusades, the Spanish Inquisition, Watergate. Now it's just mind-numbingly dull.
— Q, *Star Trek: Deep Space Nine*, "Q-Less"

I Just Dropped In To See What Condition My Condition Was In.
— Title of a popular song by Kenny Rogers and the First Edition (1967)

1.

This volume takes its title from the current project, much touted, to remove greenhouse gases from the atmosphere so as to result in a "balanced net impact" on climate. It is a monumental boondoggle, as my chapter "Scrapping Green" makes clear. But this book is not primarily an attack on Net Zero and other destructive environmentalist fantasies, though they form part of its argument. Rather, I treat Net Zero as an organizing metaphor for what is occurring to

Western culture in the widest sense: the dramatic loss of general intelligence, creative vitality, sustaining humor, intimation of the spiritual, and confidence in the future. The culture as a whole, I fear, is approaching Net Zero.

Consider, for example, the transformation of our schools and universities into re-education camps and indoctrination centers; the Sovietization of the press and vast segments of the Internet under the weight of censorship and "canceling"; the catastrophic lack of fiscal restraint and prudence among Left-oriented governments; the stoking of racial distrust and hatred via Critical Race Theory; the frowning assault against wit; the denaturing of honest language; the disciplines of 'gender' ideology, along with the travesty of "gender confirmation surgery," especially with regard to young children encouraged to "transition," and the turning males into females; and, as noted, the phony theory of man-made Global Warming—these are all aspects of a real Net Zero culture.

It is astonishing to observe the degree to which the culture has become decoupled from its traditional purlins in history, morality, faith, scientific accomplishment, artistic endeavor and plain common sense. The intuitive "feel" of the normal has now become unnatural—destabilized, confused, incoherent, bizarre, even grotesque. This is why, barring the miracle of a new "Golden Age," our future as a free people and, from a greater supervening standpoint, as a civilization has grown increasingly precarious. The drift toward critical denouement, toward a life among the ruins, seems inexorable to some. Its ETA cannot be precisely determined, but it is, on the historical calendar, uncomfortably close.

Several years ago, the noted psycholinguist and educationalist Frank Smith delivered a lecture at Brigham Young University, where I was guesting, in which he argued that the cultural Titanic was foundering and we should all jump ship. The problem, I countered, so far as I could see, was that there was nowhere to jump. Everything is the Titanic. The Titanic is the Titanic. The lifeboats are the

Titanic. The sea is the Titanic. The land is the Titanic. Even the iceberg is the Titanic. Perhaps a thin spit of coastline, a promontory or an island of reason, might gradually emerge from the turbulence—what Charles Eisenstein in *The Coronation: Essays from the Covid Moment* calls "communities of sanity" —but meanwhile the only option is to work the pumps, as it were, to keep the ship afloat.

In this regard, I would draw readers' attention to one of the great poems of the language, Alfred, Lord Tennyson's Arthurian sequence, *Idylls of the King*. By upholding the values of truth, sincerity and faith, the Arthurian knights engage with the task of holding back the tide of cynicism, depravity, disorder and self-indulgent carousing threatening to engulf the world around them. The poem was composed over a period of 25 years a century and a half before the concept of Net Zero would appear on the radar, but Net Zero *in the pejorative sense* was what Tennyson feared, as many of us do today. "The old times may be dead when every morning brought a noble chance and every chance brought out a noble." Holding the line is a strenuous venture, a way of recovering the future.

As PJM columnist Lincoln Brown writes concerning the modern age, "Even those myths created in the 20th and 21st centuries that ostensibly replaced Arthur and his knights have been co-opted to serve the ego. Witness the collapse of Star Wars and the bastardization of Middle Earth, to name two. There is no requirement that one undertake labor for one's community or even oneself. Heroes are no longer welcome. Zeroes are preferred. Zeroes, after all, are easy to mollify and manipulate."

These are affairs of great import, yet a spirit of laughter, of not taking oneself as overly earnest or self-important, needs equally to be upheld. One thinks of Monty Python's hilarious spoofing in The Holy Grail of the same Arthurian legends embraced by Tennyson. Tim the Enchanter is John Cleese's version of Tennyson's Sir Bedivere. One can be both impish and serious. The point is that Net Zero is not where we want to find ourselves. A culture in which there are no more cakes and ale is not where we want to live. There must be pleasure. At the same time, a life where the silver cord is loosed, or the golden bowl is broken, or the pitcher broken at the fountain, or the wheel broken at the cistern is not a prospect we should entertain with equanimity. There must be seriousness of intention, too. It's a subtle distinction that needs to be appreciated.

For when a free society agrees to the surrender of its freedoms and proceeds to concentrate on the relatively inane in the process of its dismemberment—let's call it bed and circuses, when it cedes its beliefs and values to the reign of a gaggle of so-called experts and cultural curators deficient in both integrity and cerebral power, when it is both pretentious and silly in equal proportions, we are witnessing a failure of collective intelligence and a sapping of social character, a wasting disease that must be properly diagnosed and meaningfully addressed if it is ever to be corrected.

Patrick Brantlinger's *Bread and Circuses: Theories of Mass Culture as Social Decay*, despite its leftist camber, is a salient book in the present context, functioning as an attempt to revise and correct the classicist thesis that the past is often superior to the present, that progress is not always for the better and very often for the worse, and that mass culture leads inevitably to decay. This is what he calls "negative classicism" or "classicist nostalgia," a prepossession that must be countered. For Brantlinger, what it boils down to is mass culture good, classical culture bad. Classicist nostalgia does not take into account or promote the "prosperity, justice and freedom" of the "alienated masses and the Third World," but somehow "contributes to the decadence and barbarism that it seems to deplore."

Brantlinger is important not because he is especially insightful but because he lays out the leftist thesis in its essence. He would have no commerce with Matthew Arnold's celebrated precepts in *Culture and Anarchy* that the educated individual and the evolved culture should commit to "the study of perfection," "the best that has been thought and said," and the landscape of thought shaped by the "great ideas." Brantlinger would not regard the labor and legacy of ancestral thought with its focus on merit and substance as an issue serious enough to inhibit the "desire, wisdom and courage" to "leap across the abyss that separates one world from another." But he never succeeds in describing what that new, emancipated, revitalized world, one which improves the lot of the masses, would look like.

My argument here is that the pivotal issue is really one of reconciliation between high and low, between classical liberalism and mass culture, between Brantlinger and Arnold, but without discounting the fact we do, in fact, live in an age of mammoth historical ignorance, prosaic triteness, a belief in fictions such as anthropogenic climate change and diverse utopian ideologies, endemic infantilism, dour feminism, and, aside from advanced digital technology, negligible accomplishment in scholarship, the arts and the sciences.

Indeed, the element of what we might call *fantasticality* is now a prominent feature of the Western psyche, serious conviction having been largely supplanted by the kind of zealous frivolity we find, for example, in a Danny Kaye-like army of eco-celebrants, leftist apparatchiks, academic elitists, and DEI saints-in-the-making, all marching in robotic unison and chanting together the risible mantras of global warming, lurking pandemics, white supremacy, alt-right violence and toxic masculinity, elevating such idiocies and chimeras to the level of dogma, and twaddle to the level of Holy Writ.

In short, we are not paying attention to the real world. We have come to resemble the citizens of Saint Augustine's city of Hippo, about whom Lewis Mumford writes in *The City in History*. They were too busy attending the games in the local Forum to defend themselves against the Vandals at the walls, with the inevitable result that the walls were breached, the city razed, and these distracted citizens put to the sword. Analogously, the public atrium today is infested with fraudsters, prigs and moralizers who have become unintentionally ridiculous and eerily oblivious to the real world around them.

This is a people who have entered the realm of Net Zero. This is a people become profoundly superficial, "unutterably dull."

2.

What, then, is to be done about our condition? "The Cultured Thug," a collection of speeches and reviews by the late conservative intellectual Jonathan Bowden, is an indispensable book for our day, developing the idea of how to reverse cultural decline. "Truthfully, in this age," Bowden wrote, "those with intellect have no courage and those with some modicum of physical courage have no intellect. If things are to alter during the next fifty years," he continued, "then we must re-embrace Byron's ideal: the cultured thug."

A jesting way of proposing something serious. The Byronic hero first made his appearance in Byron's narrative poem "Childe Harold's Pilgrimage," a figure whose nature is brooding, melancholy and scornful but capable of bravery, affection and judgment. The Byronic hero, or cultured thug, seeks to marry together the virtues of intelligence and courage, thought and action, the rarest of combinations, but one absolutely necessary in times typified by pervasive banality and fecklessness of purpose. This is the "warrior" who can make a difference. Byron describes the archetype in Canto I of the poem. "For this was not that open, artless soul/That feels relief by bidding sorrow flow, but one who sees through the flatterers of the festal hour;/The heartless parasites of present cheer."

A fun fact: Q in the *Star Trek* series, actor John de Lancie who played the role reveals, was modeled on the Byronic hero as an "enigmatic being who challenges the established order, often displays a disdain for authority and conventional morality, [and is] characterized by his existential introspection." The Byronic hero is a Q-like character, a mischievous expression of autonomy, self-reliance, defiance, humor and power, the "cultured thug" we are in need of today. In both his playfulness and his authority, he is what we might call the abrasive genius, the type of that small platoon of political and cultural leaders who can work to reverse the trend to Net Zero.

We know who they are. They are those who seek to repair an educational system in complete disarray, recognizing that while China teaches its kids calculus, our educators teach our kids gender pronouns. They are those who strive to rescue an economy that is sinking by the hour into the primordial bog. They deal decisively with a culture of intellectual lightweights, comic book characters and lazy pilgarlics who pride themselves on being Woke. They are the Constitutional warriors who wish to rebuild the major institutions on which cultural health depends. They are those with a shrewd sense of humor and a disparaging wit. They are those who struggle against the odds, however formidable, to prevent the disintegration of the nation. They are those whom the profoundly superficial feel threatened by and can do little but mock and defame. They are those like President Donald Trump, a Byronic hero on the national stage, the Q of American politics. They are those whom the Net Zero people love to hate.

The reality principle, however, must be recognized. Whether the Trumpian revolution, the new "Golden Age," comes to pass and to persist into the future remains an open question. Might it not be reversed by a subsequent electoral victory of the criminal left and a contrary flurry of executive actions reversing the gains of the current administration? Will the lower courts strive to limit the president's discretion to pursue and administer his own policies, as seems very much the case?

Moreover, the Trumpian revolution has yet to make landfall in Keir Starmer's U.K. and the commonwealth nations like Canada, Australia and New Zealand, and much of the authoritarian European Union where the anti-democratic, Net Zero dispensation continues politically dominant. It has been said that Trump is not only a president but a veritable legend, and the issue is now whether so swashbuckling a legendary figure and his knights errant can effect a radical change in the political culture so that, to quote Bowden again, we can become "heroic about your own nation, your own culture, its own history, your own ethnicity." Will America recover its mojo, will other nations see the light? Such are the stakes that are being weighed in what is nothing less than a world-historical struggle for the soul of the West, a struggle that admits of no elisions of conscience.

My overall subject is what Bowden called *metapolitics*, in other words, "the politics of culture," especially in the West, where "people are ashamed and embarrassed and self-estranged from their own culture." The essay/chapters in this book represent an effort to shed light on various manifestations of Net Zero, to out the preposterous caricatures that sully the national temper, and to analyze the critical issues that beset a profoundly superficial people, which is to say, mainly those who adhere to the dogmas of the left or are indifferent to the lessons of history.

1
THE TATTOO

Tattoos are not new. What is new is their ubiquity and extent of body coverage. They meet the eye with livid starkness everywhere one looks, turning the atmosphere and the culture positively fluorescent. What was once a niche market has expanded exponentially. According to the *New York Post* (February 14, 2025), nearly a third of American adults have a tattoo, including 22% who have more than one. Practically everyone of a certain age group, say, late teens to early fifties, seems to flaunt these decorative glyphs and totems on every visible part of their bodies, including the head and face. (Actress Amanda Bynes and rapper Post Malone are celebrity examples.) And judging from my experience in the change room of the gym where I work out, these chromatic blemishes, particle illustrations of a much wider significance, appear on the less visible parts of a person's anatomy as well.

It's a phenomenon that continues to puzzle me. Every era, of course, is marked by its own fashion anomalies once considered normative or appealing, which we often tend to regard as quaint, ridiculous, garish or merely amusing—to take just one example, the dandyism of red waistcoats, green wigs and blue hair in 19ᵗʰ Century Paris. Today is no exception, though we need not look back in time to find them absurd or grotesque. How one can appraise sumptuary excesses like the fade cut, pink hair, septum rings, tongue studs, navel piercings, and the prevalence of the orgulous tattoo as in any way attractive boggles the mind.

As the *World Journal of Psychiatry* points out in a methodological case study focusing on statistical distributions and issues relating to epidemiology, tattoos were traditionally associated with deviance and psychopathology, typically criminals, gang members and "others belonging to marginalized and counter-cultural groups." (One recalls those Grade B gangster films featuring Russian mafia members, their arms, backs and chests slathered with lurid insignia rankings.) The tattoo serves "to align the wearer with a specific group," offering comfort, protection and a collective identity. Tattoos are often also used as a kind of rebus meant to "bolster low self-esteem" or "repair a crippled self-image" or buttress an insecure individuality.

Some analysts believe that tattoos serve an ultimate evolutionary purpose rooted in sexual selection. The "human canvas" theory postulates that tattooing is an expression of human culture and "symbolic thought," with skin art developed "as a means to illustrate one's personal story." The "upping the ante" theory "suggests that tattoos evolved as a fitness indicator, enhancing one's appearance in the context of intersexual competition." In either case, the tattoo was clearly a male emblem inscribed on the flesh of the suitor and intended to interest the female prize, who could read his history and appreciate his vigor.

Starting in the 1980s, tattooing gradually became a mainstream phenomenon as a means of personal expression and as an opportunity "to explore core aspects of self-identity." The authors of the psychiatric study isolate five different motivating factors behind the increasingly popular phenomenon: identity-based personal narrative; group solidarity; embellishment of "the body as a fashion accessory;" a "badge that reflects pain tolerance and physical endurance, as a means of emphasizing sexuality [or] as an affiliation with a religious or spiritual tradition;" and an impulse enacted "for no specific reason." The tattoo is no longer sex-specific, with women flaunting skin art and regarding their bodies as an epidermal canvas almost to the same degree as men—perhaps as another foray into patriarchal territory. Bikers and felons are no longer conspicuous in the mix. Younger people in particular tend to see tats as rendering them sexy or painting them rebellious. But there is more to it than that.

French philosopher Gilles Lipovetsky in *The Empire of Fashion: Dressing Modern Democracy* argues that standards of dress and self-presentation are assertions of individual autonomy; "the cult of novelty promotes a feeling of independent individuality . . . becomes a source of discovery, of subjective positioning . . . a little adventure of the self." The individual decides to free himself or herself from the tacit rules of tradition. "[O]n the occasion of each shift in fashion," he continues, "there is a feeling, however tenuous, of subjective freedom, of liberation from past habits." A new fashion statement is thus an expression of "the individual mastery of the self," shedding the manacles of the "ancestral legacy." When not imposed by the totalitarian state as a uniform that erases differences between people, the fashion statement, according to Lipovetsky, becomes a cultural value that finds its "apotheosis in the democratic state," affirming difference and consecrating the "private personality."

Yet, the irony is inescapable. As Alexis de Tocqueville wrote in *Democracy in America*, "in democratic ages even those who are not alike are bent on becoming so and copy each other." The absolute power of the majority which distinguishes democratic epochs, Tocqueville feared, may have a dampening effect on thought, "thus extinguishing intellectual freedom." In trying to be different, we all become the same, a herd of individuals sporting the same ideas, the same tastes, the same mullet or fade, the same bell-bottom trousers, the same body piercings, the same ideological fashions, the same fondness for tattoos.

Here, as noted, Lipovetsky takes partial issue with Tocqueville, claiming that the "epidemic of mimesis" still permits people more freedom than times when "religions and traditions attempted to produce a seamless homogeneity of collective beliefs." Lipovetsky's thesis is moot; his book was published in 1994, three years after the collapse of the Soviet Union in 1991, and two years after Francis Fukuyama's *The End of History and the Last Man*, when the belief in the ascendancy of Western liberal democracy was at its zenith. Now we see that the Soviet Union did not collapse but spread its tentacles into every corner of Western culture, that the ideal of coercive and exclusionary "social justice" has obliterated the principles of merit, competence, honest justice, freedom of speech and intellectual autonomy, and that socialism is once again making a robust comeback. Tocqueville's warnings would appear to supersede Lipovetsky's hopes.

What has this to do with the remarkable proliferation of tattoo culture? In one of my more facetious moments I speculated that the tattoo in its current manifestation may be the contemporary equivalent of the Mark of Cain. Genesis 4:15 reads in part: *And the* LORD *said unto him, Therefore whosoever slayeth Cain, vengeance shall be taken on him sevenfold. And the* LORD *set a mark upon Cain, lest any finding him should kill him.*

It is not clear precisely what this mysterious mark might have been: a sign, a seal, a brand, an omen, leprosy, an aura, the Tetragrammaton itself. The *Kabbalah* suggests that the mark may have been a letter of the Hebrew alphabet intended to ward off harm, perhaps the letter vav (ו) the binding token, the divine ampersand. If there is a subliminal recognition or underlying fear pervading the culture that we are at risk, that the values on which the life of the West is predicated are rapidly deteriorating, that we inhabit an era of social and economic insecurity, then perhaps we are unconsciously seeking some means of protection from the threats that surround

us. The tattoo that paradoxically "marks" both individual uniqueness and group solidarity becomes a sign of our salvation, the gift
of a transcendent power. Though, as Harold Bloom asks in *Omens
of Millennium*, why is it these days that presumably transcendent experience seems a specialty of believers in "dank quackeries"? These
quacks view the world as what the 2nd Century Gnostics called
"the kenoma, or cosmological emptiness, a world of repetitive time,
meaningless reproduction, futurelessness."

This is obviously a fanciful conjecture—and yet the problem
remains of how to account for so unprecedented a pandemic of
pictograms, ink splotches, gothic images, names, letterings, therio-
morphic effigies, esoteric icons and various indescribable macula-
tions inscribed on foreheads, limbs, torsos and more discreet parts.
I think of the mad painter Frenhofer in Honoré de Balzac's *Le Chef
d'oeuvre inconnu* (*The Unknown Masterpiece*), who believes he is depict-
ing something beautiful but whose canvas is an unintelligible swirl
of florid pigments and tangled arabesques.

Ray Wronsov in *The Mark of Cain: The Aesthetic Superiority of
the Fashionable* takes a fascist view of the extravagances of fashion,
treating the Mark of Cain as something like the Mark of the Beast in
Revelation, but in this case a laudable banner under which the bearers
of beauty, strength and originality "exclude and torment the unwor-
thy." Wronsov would regard the omnipresent tattoo as a symbol of
the powerful and elect determined to set themselves off from the
commonplace and ultimately to eliminate those considered weak,
ugly and ordinary. His theory is also a fanciful notion but, in its less
bloodthirsty manifestation, would imply that the tattoo is the sign
of the new patriciate, the cultural elite, the *beau monde*—quite literally, the glitterati who embody Lipovetsky's consummate ethos of
aristocratic privilege.

But also, perhaps, *pace* Wronsov, of its opposite, that is, of the
rejection of self and of the need to be controlled, relieved of responsibility, to erase personal identity and serve a master. The Bill

and Melinda Gates Foundation, for example, has funded the development of biocompatible near-infrared quantum dots delivered to the skin by microneedle patches that record vaccination status, "markings" that should persist for at least 5 years, according to solar light photobleaching studies. University of Michigan epidemiologist Nicolas Hulscher refers to this tracking device as the "Mark of the Beast," a subcutaneous version of the tattoo signifying helplessness, a kind of medullary passion to be dominated by a powerful superior, similar to the Stockholm Syndrome.

By all accounts tattoos are not a benign phenomenon. They can expose their bearers to HIV/Aids and Hepatitis C. Tattoos can affect the way a body sweats, causing loss of electrolytes. They accentuate the risk of toxicological infection and, according to *The Lancet* for May 21, 2024, enhance the possibility of melanoma and basal cell carcinoma by a risk factor of 21 percent. Pregnancy and weight gain can lead to tattoo distortion. As plastic surgeon Cormac Joyce writes, tattooing "involves the integration of metallic salts and organic dyes into the dermal layer of the skin," which may produce "malignant transformation." Metabolites, the intermediate products of metabolic reactions catalyzed by various enzymes that naturally occur within cells, were detected in the bloodstream shortly after tattooing began. Studies in Germany's Federal Institute for Risk Assessment (BfR) reported that "tattoo ink pigments can accumulate in lymph nodes, potentially exposing the immune system to chemicals that may be considered toxic."

Justin Caba in *Medical Daily* notes the rise of what is called "tattoo regret" and "tattoo remorse," especially in light of its difficulty of removal and its sometimes permanence. As people grow older or gain in maturity, they may come to realize the indignity, deformity and hazard associated with the tattoo. One recalls the warning in *Leviticus* 19:28, *Ye shall not make any cuttings in your flesh for the dead, nor print any marks upon you: I am the* LORD. The passage may be more appropriate than one might think.

Nonetheless, the tattoo persists as a sign of the times. It is not merely a moderately popular eccentricity or cutaneous affectation, which in itself or as a single instance need not be offensive. But in whatever way its extraordinary prominence and body coverage may be interpreted, it strikes me as a chiefly tribal phenomenon involving the carpeting of the body on the assumption that such overlays function as a species of armor or a web of apotropaic patterns—that is, signs intended to parry or deflect evil influences—or a narrative of the self graven in a visible medium. Such figures or devices may come to the fore when a culture senses the loss of authentic identity or begins to suspect it has no right to exist, that it is subject to the curse of erasure. Tattoos represent an attempt to impose meaning in a worried recognition that meaning has gone out of the culture. We live in a time of dark intuitions, a time of endings, in which the integrated and substantial self is eroding under the corrosive effect of the loss of historical confidence, of gender fluidity, runaway multiculturalism, political correctness, vast educational deficits like so-called "discovery learning" and the rise of collectivist ideology. Like Cain, we are under threat for our complicity in an act of violence—call it culturcide.

In such times a generation may strive to mark itself as singular and separate, as an assembly of heroic individuals reminiscent of Nietzsche's Übermensch rising above the "last man" of a dying culture—fighting the recognition that they are themselves these "last men." They see themselves as the initiates of the future, as special cases, as different from the common ruck, as "marked out," as deserving of redemption, as unique and distinctive. In the wake of Donald Trump's victory in the 2024 election, female members of the intersectional church began to tat their wrists blue to signify their socialist, pro-Democrat, anti-Trump status. As one of these unstable women averred, tattoos were "more permanent, more serious" as distinguishing signs than wearable markers. But this phenomenon is merely a political twist or digression in a larger story.

For we are dealing with a generation that has little to distinguish itself apart from the external excrescences of bark art, signalling an unmerited estimation of the self. Such ostensible badges of uniqueness are really emblems of desperation and one-dimensional replicas of mundane sameness, in effect, disfigurements that betoken a suspicion of weakness and vulnerability, and of the need for protection.

In this context, one thinks of Philip Rieff's *My Life among the Deathworks* where Rieff distinguishes between three types of culture: the culture of paganism, in which fate and perpetual threat were the dominant motifs and people sought to protect themselves against the wayward and unpredictable gods, "a constant energy of menace," by observing taboos; the culture of the Abrahamic religions, in which faith in a divine legislator and benefactor rather than fate is the determining factor; and the culture of modernity, in which what he calls an "officer class" of artists, academics and intellectuals control a world devoid of a sacred order, of a truth consensus, and of inherent meaning. In such a world emptied of tradition and an accepted moral order, the individual is cast upon his own resources, which are insufficient to withstand the hazards and terrors of existence. The tendency of the current generation is thus to return to the first, pagan culture and shield itself from the chaos and contingency of an arbitrary and frightening world by observing a system of salvific taboos, reified visibly as tattoos.

What a tale a tattoo tells! Admittedly, my reading of a cultural contagion is merely a rarefied hypothesis, yet it may enjoy a degree of plausibility. It may be argued that in the absence of spiritual depth and intellectual substance, these stamped epitomes of a culture *in extremis* seek to establish an epidermal identity as the only psychic option remaining to them. In a time of historical amnesia and hedonistic excess, they call attention to a population in thrall to emptiness through an emblazoned superficiality. Who knows? The Lord moves in mysterious ways. Perhaps these ciphers may be saved. They bear the Mark.

2

GOOD FENCES
MAKE GOOD CITIZENS

The first time I met Jordan Peterson, we disagreed. He had just delivered a brilliant talk for the Society for Academic Freedom and Scholarship (SAFS), treating in part of the pros and cons of Liberal and Conservative political philosophy. Where we disagreed entailed what he considered the pejorative side of Conservatism. Peterson argued that Conservative thinking and practice were a noble endeavor, but regrettably focused on the concept of walls, a kind of insularity that tended to exclude much that was regarded as disruptive or troubling to a sense of unanimity and epistemological coherence; indeed, such novel intrusions were likely to be regarded as a species of "disease." There could be something closed-minded about Conservative principles, a rejection of the strange, the innovative, the foreign, and the revitalizing effect of infusions from elsewhere.

Such a thesis seemed odd coming from a culture hero known for his courage in rejecting social justice groupthink and promoting the notion of personal obligation as a counterweight to runaway "rights." True, as Peterson wrote in *12 Rules for Life: An Antidote to Chaos*, as if in contradiction to half his title, "chaos, possibility, growth and adventure" add to the intensity and meaningfulness of life, situating us "on the border between order and chaos." But one must be careful how much chaos one lets cross the border into the constitutional order of both the self and the culture—and of the polity as well. As times have shown, the core Liberal/Left agenda of open borders (or as we now call it, globalism), in the realms of both practical life and ideological consensus, is an invitation to discord and misrule.

The segue from Peterson's remarks is a salient one. New elements are entering not only the nation but the culture as well, an injection of novelty that is not, *pace* Peterson, an invigorating but a destabilizing influence. The breaching of the southern border by a torrent of illegal migrants, as everyone who is still compos knows, is an unprecedented disaster. A nation without border controls is no longer a nation but a theme park "justified" by Liberal/Left pre-conceptions, a kind of free-for-all Disney World made for kids and juveniles in which the rides and features gradually cease to work. A Magic Kingdom Park minus the magic, it is an anarchist's wet dream and the dystopian project of the political Left. Chaos breaches the frontiers.

The rupture at the border is also a symbol of the widening fissures in traditional culture—the beliefs, assumptions, usages and norms we once took for granted. One recalls Leonard Cohen's brilliant song "*Anthem*" where he sings of the "crack where the light gets in," a musical rendering of Peterson's observations—which turns out to be in far too many cases, notwithstanding my old and honored friend, a rift where the darkness gets in. And the Left, as history has proven, brings political and cultural darkness wherever it has prevailed.

Dennis Prager has written what amounts to an obituary for the nation and the modern West: "Everything the Left touches it ruins." He scrolls down the list of disciplines, monuments, democratic entitlements, social structures and institutions that have crumbled as the cultural barriers that once "conserved" the nation and its people have been levelled: art, music, journalism, education, the family, childhood, race relations, sexual differentiation, the military, sports, the First Amendment, all have been rendered derelict, all now signs of "the great American tragedy."

In an article titled "Third Worldizing America," Victor Davis Hanson similarly points to the "crimes" of the Left, the "utter breakdown of the law," and the dissolution of the conceptual borders of the country sponsored by historical distortions like the *1619 Project*. As he writes in *The Dying Citizen*, "Citizens differ from visitors, aliens, and residents passing through who are not rooted inside borders where a constitution and its laws reign supreme." For a nation to prosper, citizens "must honor the traditions and customs of our country," and recognize the necessity of "delineated and established borders" if they are not to find themselves living in a social and political wilderness. "Aliens," to use Hanson's term, whether foreign or domestic, illegal immigrants or tribal Leftists, are cultural interlopers whose influence is destructive.

Some walls must come down. Some walls must go up. Some walls keep people in. Some walls keep invaders out. Some walls are raised to prevent the truth from entering the field of public discourse, such as the mainstream media's propaganda wall erected and maintained over the decades to protect the political establishment, the "social justice" hypocrites, the oligarch class, the banking aristocracy, the administrative predators—those whom Thomas Sowell calls the "anointed." But a wall, as we understand it here, is not an Iron Curtain. A defensive wall is an immune system with a specific, beneficial function, to repel what is harmful. Of course, some walls have gates that may be opened, and should be opened, for purposes of commerce, travel, knowledge and replenishment—Peterson's "gripping and meaningful" irruptions into the citadel. The gatekeepers, however, must be responsible, informed, judicious and loyal to the people they represent and to the founding traditions of the nation. They must know when to open the gates and when to shut them. They must labor for the advantage of their citizens.

Such was the intention of the MAGA policies of the Trump administration, which worked to reinstall the supporting walls of nation and culture, that is, to aid working families, set the economy on a strong footing, with "low unemployment, and wage increases across every demographic," as Julie Kelly writes in *Disloyal Opposition*, rebuild the military, thwart a "swamp" of domestic enemies, establish a perimeter wall at the porous border and implement rational immigration protocols. An initiative of this nature is not a kind of protectionist tariff wall built to exclude new ideas or healthy competitive forces in order to profit a guild of candlemakers by prohibiting windows, as in Frédéric Bastiat's famous fable in *The Economics of Freedom*. It is, rather, an effort to retain and foster a productive national identity and a significant degree of cultural integrity while remaining proportionately open to new ventures and discoveries.

Today, things have changed for the worse. The walls, physical, moral and customary, that keep the culture intact and shield its citizens from the incursion of parasites and the derelictions of the Left have collapsed and will need to be raised again if the nation is to flourish as it once did. Citizens can no longer be indifferent to the plight of the present, as if they were members of the Church of Laodicea whom John the Elder castigated in *Revelation* (3:15) as adiabatic, as "neither hot nor cold." Citizens will need to recover their republican temperature if the community is to survive.

In *The Dark Side of the Left*, Richard J. Ellis, a Leftist paradoxically critical of the Left, is equally insistent on the necessity for national coherence. "In such a society," he writes, "the more hierarchical visions of ordered community will continue to resonate." Leftists, however, are like the magistrates in Constantine Cavafy's celebrated poem "Waiting for the Barbarians" whose gates are opened wide, and who eagerly await the arrival of the barbarians and are disappointed when they fail to appear.

What all this means, obviously, is that the wall the keeps out interlopers, illegal migrants and unwanted visitors must continue to be built or rebuilt. No less important, the interior walls of the culture that safeguard intellectual, creative, family, informational, medical, legislative, personal, market and commissary relations will need to be rebuilt. Both species of wall, material and cultural, must be erected at the same time if the nation is to be "conserved." "Good fences make good neighbors," Robert Frost's churlish neighbor in "Mending Wall," a benighted old farmer who "moves in darkness . . . like an old-stone savage," was fond of repeating. Frost was, on the whole, of the opposite persuasion:

> Something there is that doesn't love a wall,
> That wants it down.

Frost was wrong and his neighbor was largely right—certainly in the contemporary social and political context. Something there is that sometimes loves a wall, needs a wall to keep out vandals, barbarians and fifth columnists and to maintain the boundaries, external as well as internal, that allow for secure and ordered life. Good fences make good citizens.

3

ON SCENTED MINIPADS

B efore I invested in a car one of the most harrowing experiences I had to submit to daily was the rush-hour bus or metro. It wasn't the waiting in line, the hideous crush of humanity, the standing for what seemed like hours that particularly distressed me, it was the smell. There is nothing quite so devastating as the stench of coagulating deodorants. People smelled like rancid chocolate. I especially remember the cumulative shock wave of Old Spice which made my nostrils crumple like newspaper. But that was only the men. The women were in another olfactory dimension entirely. The odor of wilted gardenia was omnipresent. I would stand beside pretty young women who stank like urinal pucks of rosewater, sandalwood and antiseptic. Others smelled like perambulating lemons, acrid, with a hint of Windex lingering about their persons. It was worse in the early mornings when people reeked like corpses doused with the failed discretion of embalming fluid. Now and then there would rise in the air a suspicion of fart fledged with the ethereal plumage of Chanel or Fabergé. That was how I knew these slumped unmoving forms were still alive.

I wonder what it is we are ashamed of. Is Old Spice the child of the New Testament? Is Lady Speed Stick the lineal descendant of Pauline theology? Do all these gels and applications confess to a secret contempt for the flesh as being somehow too primitive, too pagan, too animal, too unruly, too present? We enjoy our bodies too much to give them up. A passionate fling, a pneumatic eiderdown, coffee and oranges in a sunny chair (to quote Wallace Stevens), the long, easy, meditative, peristaltic flex of the bowels—who can deny such experiences are inherently pleasurable? Yet hundreds of years of Presbyterianism are not flung aside with a Belmondo shrug. When everything has been factored out by historical analysis, there remains the guilt. The old resentment of the body continues to rankle and fester but the intransigent love of the body persists with countervailing strength. From this tension, this conflict, the cosmetics industry has always profited.

Today we need no longer splash perfumes about indiscriminately to make up for the lack of sanitary facilities. Everybody in the civilized world can enjoy at least a simple ablution at almost any moment of the day or night. One might think if there ever were a time in which deodorants should appeal to nobody but perverts, it would be right now. Yet the opposite is the case. Could the reason be that as the manifold delights of the flesh become more and more available, the endocrinology of guilt abides with us even more tenaciously. Thus the deodorant explosion. We have bodies but we don't have bodies. We become our own fragrant Gardens of Eden. We are the resurrected flesh promised by the Book of Revelation and the Koran.

The scented minipad, however, is a unique symbol of our existential condition. One can scarcely turn on the TV these days without seeing some nubile ballerina in mid-splits expatiating on the virtues of the latest in yoniwear. It reposes invisibly beneath her tutu like a hospital tuck, clean and decisive. It permits her to solve the occupational hazard of being a woman and to quell the monthly tremors of the professional ballet dancer. Not only can she perform the most strenuous of cabrioles without bleeding like a stuck pig but she even smells sweetly afterwards. Now she can be a man and a flower at the same time.

The scented minipad—to widen the conjecture—derives not only from our inheritance of guilt before the unassimilable mortification of the flesh—Original Skin, as it were—but from the apologetic dis-ease women feel before their own raw femininity. The minipad betokens the compound transgression of having not just a body but, O mater Dolorosa! a female body. Sweat, feces and menarche are difficult enough for any sensitive being to put up with, but discharge too! And so women run about in a state of aromatic nether purdah whose eventual disclosure leads to the most unfortunate of after-effects. I know of men who, following acts of glossal intimacy, have been reduced to repeated and obsessive gargling to recover the use of their taste buds. Any man who has managed to hang on to his senses would rather part an honest patch of pubic hair than enter a grove of synthetic pomegranates or visit a well-kept cemetery redolent of the ghosts of departed minipads.

There is, of course, a practical side to the scented minipad—apart from the soothing of catamenial despairs—which is more than an expression of ancestral guilt. It is also a way of disguising a more immediate one. The scented minipad is the latest flower of sin. As sex becomes less confined to the prudence of the night and grows increasingly diurnal, women must not only keep themselves on red alert but come home smelling of inoffensive lilac. They are cleansed not only of having flesh but of using it. But this is a mere quotidian advantage that does not disguise a deeper hankering for salvation.

The TV commercials reveal what it is we really long for. The verbal gush coupled with the vaginal stanch are no different in principle from the manly reticence cloaked in English Leather commanding the velocity flow of a black RX-7. This is how it will manifestly be in Heaven where we shall all enjoy the paradisiacal disembarrassment of our natural awkwardness. We shall be in total control of our fears and secretions, acting with the assurance of disembodiment. Meanwhile the Great Panegyric is flourishing as never before and the whited sepulchre, as is only proper in this day of rampant miniaturization, has become portable and ubiquitous.

4

HOW TO HAGGLE
WITH A SOCIALIST

I don't make a habit of visiting used or rare bookshops—the print museums of our digital age—but I have occasionally enjoyed book-hunting in an out-of-the-way bibliotheca, most memorably when I was living in Greece. On one of these expeditions, I had wandered in, quite by chance, to the Karaghiozis Emporium in the warrens of the Plaka, the neighbourhood at the base of the Acropolis. Despite its impressive moniker the Emporium was actually a decrepit little hovel, its name borrowed from the celebrated Turk-Greek shadow puppet-theater character—an uneducated, unemployed trickster given to risqué jokes and sharp social satire—who has delighted Greek audiences for generations. The place struck me as a kind of bookend, so to speak, to the Karaghiozis Museum in the posh Athenian suburb of Maroussi, thus bracketing the vast social disparities in Greek society while at the same time accentuating its cultural and historical unity.

The Karaghiozis Emporium was nothing more than a literal hole in the wall, a gap in a stone façade fringed by a pelmet of aluminum shutters. It was not so much a used bookstore or a rare bookstore as a rarely used bookstore. The only occupant when I entered the premises was the *affentiko* (proprietor, from the Turkish *effendi*), a grizzled dwarf who seemed a dead ringer for the rogue puppet himself. He was seated on a rather high tripod, sipping a *turkiko* (Greek coffee, adopted from the Turkish occupation) which he poured from a battered briki while scanning a much crumpled newspaper, which turned out to be the popular left wing Eleftherotypia, favoured by trade unionists, diehard communists and prospective terrorists.

He scarcely troubled to notice me as I cast a skeptical eye over the mouldering copies of socialist tracts, translations of various French anarchists, a prominently displayed Franz Fanon and, of course, the obligatory pile of Communist Manifestos and Das Kapitals, all looking distinctly worse for the machinations of that ruthless free marketeer, Time. There was also a saucer of milk and the scattered heads of *maridhes* (smelt) on the dirt floor laid out for the feral cats that would slink in for a brief repast. The *affentiko* obviously had a soft spot for the proletarians among the scavenging classes.

As he had not bothered to acknowledge me and as I could see nothing of interest among his wares, I was about to leave when I noticed, at the top of a corded bundle by the cave-like entrance, a cat-eared copy of Yannis Ritsos' *Epitaphios*, the radical poet's 1936 threnody for a worker assassinated during the Salonika general strike. This was indeed a rare find. Receiving permission to untie the parcel—permission consisted of an abrupt lowering of the head, the Greek gesture for assent—I also discovered the 1967 edition of Dinos Christianopoulos' *Poiimata* (Poems) and a loose-sheet copy, collected between cardboard panels, of Eleni Vasileiou's *Appolonia*, which I'd vaguely heard of but had never come across.

I couldn't believe my luck and immediately began the process of negotiation. Notwithstanding the advice of Canadian bookseller and author David Mason in his charming pamphlet "The Protocols of Used Bookstores" — "Do not ask for a discount" and "It is not nice to lecture the proprietor on how and why you know that the price of his book is ludicrous" —I knew that bargaining is expected and pro forma in a traditional Levantine or Greek marketplace,

which the Karaghiozis Emporium manifestly was. Now the affentiko deigned to address me and pointed to a tiny stool at the edge of
the cluttered table where I could make myself uncomfortable. And
so the haggling began, amid the yowls of cats, the incessant ham-
mering from the adjacent metal shop and the whorls of black smoke
wafting in from one passing *trikiklos* after another (3-wheeled mo-
torized carts).

Socialism may be anti-capitalist, but socialists often make the
best capitalists. So with my interlocutor. His political disposition
was no impediment to his shrewd and sinuous bargaining methods,
which included claiming that the rarity of the books was akin to
"triremes that fly over the trees at sunset," quoting one of Ritsos'
better lines from "The Dead House." This impressed me greatly,
far more than another used bookseller I had dealt with in Montreal, who quoted only prices. He then described his strenuous and
costly odyssey to obtain these coveted tomes in the scriptorium of
a monastery on Mount Athos—a most unlikely repository for a
cache of leftist volumes—and expressed an unwillingness to part
with them except to someone worthy of so precious and exquisite
an intellectual treasure. Sensing that he was attempting to compensate for his unusually short stature with an unreasonably tall price, I
feigned weary indifference, assuring him I was mainly interested in
the books as a sentimental token of my visit to the Plaka.

Moreover, I affected to have little leisure, letting it be known
that I had to stop by the shoe shop across the alleyway for a pair of
sandals before rushing to Pireaus to catch the ferry back to the island
where I was living. This was, I soon realized, too clumsy and trans-
parent a ploy to be effective, but I partially recovered lost ground by
matching his Ritsos quote with one from Giorgos Seferis' signature
poem, "In the Manner of G.S.": "Ships whistle now as night falls
on Pireaus." This earned me an involuntary grunt of approval and
an apparent willingness to bend on price, even though Seferis was
a patrician sensibility whom the bookseller would have renounced.

To press my advantage, I glanced frequently and conspicuously at my watch. He sipped his *turkiko* and grumbled beneath his breath, peering closely at the books as if he were about to cut diamonds. It didn't look like we were making much progress. Then came his crowning maneuver. He slipped from his perch behind the table and made as if to replace the books in the corner where I had found them. My face fell, rather too visibly. That was his cue.

Suddenly appearing to change his mind, he smiled benignly, as if taking pity on the poor foreigner who had only belatedly understood the immense spiritual value of the antiquarian gift he was about to forfeit, and stated his final price, the best he could do considering his daily expenses, the stray cats he had to feed, the exorbitant rent for this *spilaion* (cave), and the three daughters he had to build *prika* (dowry) houses for. My daughters, he said, quoting Ritsos again, are "at the windows, hidden behind their dreams." Despite the poetry and my growing respect for the man—which I don't grant lightly to socialists—I resisted the urge to capitulate. But eventually, after due consideration of the bookseller's dignity as well as my pocketbook, I agreed to a price that was a little higher than I'd budgeted for, and a little lower than he'd initially demanded. Like the characters in a Karaghiozis-orchestrated triumph, everyone was happy. The bookseller got his adjusted price, I luxuriated in my trove, the cats had their *maridhes* and the daughters, no doubt, could look forward to their *prika*.

But, of course, since the shoe shop was in full view directly across the way and I couldn't honourably renege on my weak transactional strategy, it also cost me a pair of sandals.

5

FOOTBALL AND FEMINISM

Let me begin by saying that I am an unapologetic patriarch who deeply appreciates female beauty and intelligence. I count among my friends women whom I admire enormously. I have a lovely and brilliant wife whom I regard as the greatest blessing of my life, as per Genesis 2:18. I say this to dispel any notion that I am a misogynist or some sort of knuckle-dragging chauvinist. That being said, I should also declare my convictions touching the gender wars tearing apart the time-honored relations between the sexes in the decadent West.

I firmly believe in the biological, psychological, and domestic differences between men and women, who are God's or Nature's determined partners in the drama of both survival and individual flourishing but occupy distinctive and natural domains commensurate with their genetically given talents, aptitudes, and strengths. We might say that men and women are binary but complementary beings. There are anomalies and "crossovers," obviously, but the general pattern is pre-ordained regardless of the theories and practices of the feminist sorority and its enablers who claim precedence under the deceptive rubric of "equality."

This basic distinction was vividly brought home to me during the five years I lived on the Greek islands. I learned many interesting things in those years—the two levels of the Greek language depending on social status, local viticulture and the unique taste of retsina, the "lift" of bouzouki, sirtaki, and chasapiko, the meditative zembekiko, the archaic power of modern Greek poetry, and, especially significant, the nature of domestic arrangements pertaining to spheres of marital influence. Broadly speaking—and this is not a cliché—men hold sway in the tavernas, women control the home.

The trade-off works exceptionally well, if at times a tad too enthusiastically. I have seen dishes fly when the men come home late and tipsy—the area between my house and my neighbor's was cobbled with broken crockery. The women, for their part, do not intrude on the rummy games and heated political discussions—every Greek man is a potential prime minister—in the sacred precinct of the taverna. But both join hand and spirit when it comes to the raising of children, on the whole, training boys and girls in their respective social roles, though allowing for individual qualities and faculties.

Relations between the sexes are mainly harmonious—if, let's say, somewhat vigorous at times—so long as the rights and privileges of each are neither resented nor confused. (There are exceptions to the rule, primarily in the big cities where a globalist or international culture has taken root, diluting the natal Greek character. This is a form of urban blight we are all familiar with.)

Marriage is not only a sacrament, elaborately celebrated but an implicit contract regarding the cultural territory discretely reserved for men and women. There are no half-female political cabinets in Greece, as there are, for example, in an effeminate nation like my own. Island Greeks, for the most part, are not interested in feminist doctrine and regard the trans phenomenon with undisguised distaste. The major sports spectacles, in particular soccer, a national pastime, are dominated by men, both on the field and in the announcer's booth. Which brings me to one of my major pleasures, namely, watching NFL football.

Football is a synecdochic expression of the essential male character, on the one hand pugnacious, rowdy and boisterous; on the other analytic, rational and problem-solving, as anyone who understands the strategic, chess-like nature of the game can attest. The element of sacrifice for the team and for the brotherhood—as is evident in the concern among opposing teams for an injured player and the post-game, fraternal ritual between winners and losers—is what binds these aspects of masculinity. It is something that feminists have never been able to come to terms with.

Since football is a man's game, I wonder what a woman referee is doing on the field. Must I endure female intra-and-post-game interviewers who have little idea what the game entails and trade mainly in inanities? Or female commentators who have never played the game expounding on its involutions beside former players and coaches sitting on the same panel—those who know firsthand and from experience what they are talking about? Having spent some time back in the day on my varsity practice squad as a free safety, I know how difficult it is to execute a proper tackle on a six-foot-four tight end hurtling toward you without breaking your neck in the process. I know when to cover zone or play the man, to join the quarterback rush, or to fake it and drop back. I recognize when the coach is calling a bonehead play. I can appreciate what is happening on the field. Most men do. And they are the ones I want to listen to when the progress of a game is being described, discussed, and analyzed.

The men, we might note, are always chivalrous and amiable to a fault in their comportment, but eye candy belongs elsewhere. It's rather a jarring spectacle, the men formal in jackets and ties, the women often looking as if they're about to paint the town red. What is a young woman wearing a bright pink, form-fitting, slant-décolleté pantsuit doing on a football panel? Carrie Underwood's dynamite performance introducing Sunday Night Football represents the extent of my appreciation for the female contribution in this context.

Of course, there are several full-pad tackle female teams, but women's football is not a truly serious game and may often resemble a comedy act, like the Lady Yellow Jackets of yore. The caliber of play exhibited by the gridiron girls bears no comparison to the skill and robustness and the ever-present threat of severe injury of male college and professional teams, any more than women's soccer or hockey comes close to the speed, intensity, and finesse—and interest—of male soccer and hockey. It's a fact that must be faced despite the ideological intent to render the masculine estate female-inclusive.

An illustration of the manly character of the game and its players is provided by a Tampa Bay Buccaneers backup quarterback Blaine Gabbert who, along with his two brothers, rescued the occupants of a helicopter that had crashed in the water. This is the sort of thing that men do, taking risks both on and off the field and doing their utmost to excel and contribute, whether in the game of football or the game of life. Of course, all human beings are flawed regardless of the distribution of chromosomes, but the slur of toxic masculinity is a feminist canard and a dogmatic libel.

This is not to say that good women do not appreciate what men do in the world—or that they do not appreciate NFL football. My wife enjoys the game and is learning, with my assistance, to understand its tactical offensive and defensive adjustments from snap to snap, the subtle disposition of configurations like the Okie Front, and, in short, its intricacies and complexities. And she, too, has had enough of the female interloper from whom we both wish to be rescued. It would take a piece of Hail Mary league legislation to rid us of the scourge. Fond hope!.

6

STEPHEN HAWKING'S
MORAL BLACK HOLE

There had been considerable fallout regarding world-re-nowned cosmologist the late Stephen Hawking's re-fusal to attend Israel's Fifth Presidential Conference on the grounds of Israeli malfeasance toward the Palestinians. Whatever one's view of the Jewish state, there should be little doubt that the physicist's decision to boycott the event was both intellectually indefensible and morally suspect. It raises the age-old question of how mental agility and moral folly can co-exist in the same person.

As several commentators have indicated, his position was indeed intellectually indefensible since Hawking evinced no knowledge of the history of the Middle East, ludicrously compared Israel to apartheid South Africa, and seemed wholly unaware of the provably fraudulent nature of the Palestinian narrative. Palestinian revisionism has falsified the historical record in practically every conceivable respect. The data are readily accessible and no genuine scholar or thinking person can deny them and still retain a modicum of integrity.

At the same time, his attitude was morally suspect owing to the fact that Hawking, who suffered from motor neuron disease, would have been rendered mute without the advances and advantages of Israeli medical breakthroughs. Nitsana Darshan-Leitner, director of

Shurat HaDin–Israel Law Center, called Hawking's boycott hypocritical. "His whole computer-based communication system runs on a chip designed by Israel's Intel team. I suggest that if he truly wants to pull out of Israel, he should also pull out his Intel Core i7 from his tablet."

In a stinging article for *FrontPage Magazine*, Ari Lieberman pointed to the sharp distinction between the benefits and gifts that Israel has lavished upon mankind in science, technology and medicine and the deficits and depravities that are the legacy of the Arab world: barbarism, cultural regression, ignorance, religiously sanctioned violence and terroristic savagery. It is a distinction, we should have thought, that a world-class scientist like Hawking—who, incidentally, had visited Iran without uttering a single criticism of that rogue state—should have been equipped to make but was clearly unable to do.

This is not an argument against Hawking's uniquely cerebral brilliance, though his belief in man as a cognitive machine is far from convincing. Admittedly, his conception of M-theory or model-dependent reality, formulated in his monumental *The Grand Design*, that asserts there is "no single mathematical model or theory that can describe every aspect of the world" but rather a "network of theories," is provocative and merits considering. Nonetheless, physicist Wolfgang Smith in his *Science & Myth* shows how Hawking's book is, in the final analysis, a "baseless and amateurish speculation" akin to a pseudo-philosophy. For example, Hawking refutes the concept of intelligent design by affirming it, that is, he asserts that "a wide sense of cosmic architecture" is superior to the earlier geocentric model of the universe because it is "reflective of intelligence." You can't have it both ways.

Additionally, Smith points out in *The Quantum Enigma* that intentional acts cannot be reduced to the unpredictable behavior of sub-atomic particles in the firing of cortical neurons. Stochastic to the core, "Quantum mechanics contradicts the long-standing canon of Laplacean determinism," which Hawking asserts as a given. Even a great scientist, it appears, can be blinded by his own renown.

One recalls his most celebrated theory, namely, that black holes leak radiation, but he could not register the lies, obsessions and hatreds that routinely leak from the black hole of the Islamic world—perhaps "gush" would be the more accurate word. Of course, we need to make an adjustment here in the interest of precision: what are emitted from the Islamic world are not photons but, say, crepusculons, not particles of light, as in the original theory, but particles of darkness.

Hawking, then, could countenance the retrograde policies, Jew-hatred and terror-sponsorship of Iran, a country to which he granted legitimacy with his approving visit. But when it came to the democratic nation whose medical and technological discoveries had given him a new lease on life, he engaged in facile and politically correct posturing. "One cannot really argue with a mathematical theorem," Hawking had asserted, but one can surely argue with a political assumption—and Hawking's was defective at best and invidious at worst.

Hawking's profound failings as a social and political thinker are a subset of a much larger syndrome—the naivety or ineptitude of an acknowledged genius when he (or she) proceeds to pontificate on matters beyond their specialized field and insist on addressing the affairs of the world in general. It appears to be an occupational hazard that plagues a substantial number of such cynosures. This is not quite the same thing as the infirmity that afflicts the "expert," insofar as an "expert" can be frequently relied upon to botch, mishandle, degrade or obfuscate the very area in which his "expertise" presumably applies. The maladroit "genius," on the contrary, is one who is lambently at home in his domain, though not outside of it.

In a second article for Frontpage, Lieberman touched on the notion of the idiot savant, who "typically lack[s] normal social communication skills but possesses an abnormally high skill in such isolated disciplines as mathematics or art." He is a personality that is "very easily manipulated." Lieberman dismisses the idea in Hawking's case, but I would not be so hasty. I tend to regard Hawking as, let us say, a useful idiot savant, for by his determination to boycott the Israeli symposium, he not only stigmatized Israel but reinforced the convictions and sentiments of antisemites and anti-Zionists (often one and the same thing) around the world and across the disciplines. In any event, the category of specialized and selectively brilliant incompetents remains intact and boasts a prestigious membership. These are people whom Daniel Flynn calls, in a book of that title "intellectual morons," gifted persons who squander their talent by pronouncing on questions beyond their level of personal competence on the grounds of some sort of personal supremacy, a standard deviation self-affirmation. To mention just a few as illustrations:

Bobby Fischer, arguably the greatest chess player who ever lived, was consumed by absurd conspiracy theories and irrational hatreds. Einstein was a political naïf; if he could have had his way, Israel would never have been born as the unitary State of Israel (and Hawking wouldn't have profited from the microprocessors that permitted him to communicate). Celebrated Jewish philosopher Martin Buber who lived and taught in Israel, basking in nationwide acclaim, actually justified the Palestinian Arab pogroms of 1921, 1929 and the late 30s, urging that desperate Jewish holocaust refugees be permitted to enter Palestine only with Arab permission. Richard Dawkins, a renowned biologist, has little understanding of the moral universe. It all comes down for him to the power of the genes and the absence of the Lord, a thesis that empties the human world of moral choice and freedom of the will while dictating ex cathedra to the mystery of the Creation: it is inappropriate for a scientist to assert that God does not exist since that statement can be neither proved nor falsified. It is equally an act of pure hubris.

Martin Heidegger, considered by many the greatest philosopher of the 20th century, was an unrepentant Nazi. Bertrand Russell urged Britain to surrender to the same regime that Heidegger supported. In *The Flight from Truth: The Reign of Deceit in the Age of Information*, Jean-François Revel cites a 1937 speech in which Russell declared that "Britain should disarm, and if Hitler marched his troops into this country when we were undefended, they should be welcomed like tourists and greeted in a friendly way." In his essay "Reflections on Ghandi," George Orwell records the Mahatma's answer to the Jewish predicament in the 1940s: "Ghandi's view was that the German Jews ought to commit collective suicide, which 'would have aroused the world and the people of Germany to Hitler's violence' . . . When, in 1942, he urged non-violent resistance against a Japanese invasion, he was ready to admit that it might cost several million deaths." Ghandi was a leader of the Indian National Congress and a promoter of independence from British rule, in other words, a domestic politician, who had no compunction in advising the Jews trapped in the European slaughterhouse to submit to their extinction.

Similarly, many Nobel Laureates have dismal and even reprehensible track records. One thinks of the ferocious antisemitism of José Saramago and the petulant and sophomoric anti-Americanism of Harold Pinter. Celebrated Greek composer of oratorios Mikis Theodorakis, candidate for the 2000 Nobel, may be a musical genius but he is also a gutter antisemite. Economist Paul Krugman, who is much in the news, may know his Keynes but he certainly does not know how the real world works, arguing for increased government debt and the immateriality of deficits because "we owe what we have borrowed to ourselves." As it happens, we also owe it to China, and owing to ourselves makes little sense in an interconnected world without which we could not be our economic selves. This lionized resolver of our fiscal ills will not rest until the nation goes bankrupt, or in the words of William Anderson, a member of the Austrian School of Economics, "his central message is this: internal bond finance of government trumps scarcity." Scarcity is a fact of the real world that impinges on the life of real people, not a conceptual fancy that exists inside a theoretical construct or the addled head of a New York Times economist.

Former U.S. Secretary of Energy Steven Chu would win a prize for world-class buffoonery if one were instituted. Chu, who was awarded a Nobel for his work in laser cooling, is a great fan of glucose and termite guts to reduce the world's dependence on oil. He has recommended painting roofs and roads white to reflect sunlight and save money on air conditioning. He was also a chief promoter of the Solyndra fiasco, costing the American taxpayer over half a billion dollars. Noam Chomsky is the acclaimed founder of a transformational-generative linguistic discipline so complex that few people understand it, yet he is a committed socialist who is punitively pro-Covid mandates, vehemently anti-American, pro-Palestinian and virulently anti-Israel.

The list could be extended indefinitely. "Great men" may be great in their professional endeavors but, all too often, when they range outside the borders of their specialties they manifest either as downright silly or positively dangerous. These are very smart people, but they are "hawking" dubious wares. High intelligence counts for little in the sociocultural realm when it is confined to the narrow if intricate space of a singular curriculum or specialization, when it is not leavened by common sense and moral clarity, or when it considers itself, by virtue of its disciplinary eminence, as authoritative in pronouncing on complex and recalcitrant questions outside its particular field of study.

One recalls the Latin mortuary aphorism *De mortuis nil nisi bonum dicendum est*—Of the dead nothing but good is to be said—indicating that it is unseemly to speak ill of the dead who cannot defend or justify themselves. Nevertheless, it is an adage that must on many occasions be honored in the breach. Observations are not epitaphs. As for Hawking, a representative figure of this strange breed mantled in adulation, he may have been a great scientist and a suffering human being, but he was also, like many of his congeners, an igno-ramus and a moral imbecile. Why should we be surprised?

7

THE ADS TELL
THE STORY

In *Against the Great Reset*, Harry Stein asks how the Left has managed to subvert the culture and trample so effectively upon the fundamental concepts of decency, equality, justice, morality and even human biology itself, not to mention humor and modesty. The answer may be found not only in policy and power wielded from the top but in the gradual saturation of the public mind with a vast set of implicit assumptions regarding what constitutes enlightened societal advancement. In other words, a large part of the answer is the Left's near-absolute domination of mass popular culture—music, film, sports, news media, entertainment and so on—all infused with the values and conventions that reflect the progressivist worldview. "We have been slow to recognize," Stein writes, "the extent to which the culture has been weaponized against us."

To take only one such instance of social manipulation, consider the ads that punctuate every TV program from game shows, sitcoms, crime series, dramas, documentaries and sports events. What we are observing is another form of Vance Packard's "hidden persuaders," promos not only selling a product by attaching it to associated images of glamor or accomplishment or by flashing subliminal messages, as Packard documented, but by introducing new social norms associated with the dogmas of "social justice," identity politics, racial preferences and gender equity.

Thus, many of these ads while touting a product will feature gay and lesbian couples, sometimes even with kids. A Toyota car commercial features a lesbian couple followed by a mixed racial couple followed by a gay couple, all enthusing over the latest model. The appeal is not merely to a small consumer group of so-called marginals but to the white liberal conscience. These squibs will show gracile women working heavy machinery and driving macho trucks, or clever women instructing clueless young men how to grow their incomes. They will show gormless white men being humiliated by savvy black men, as in the FanDuel betting ads. Even Captain America is now black, though according to the U.S. Census Bureau, blacks make up only 13.7 percent of the American population. Grossly overweight people, particularly women, are featured to promote the ideological fetish of "body positivity."

Moreover, a plurality of ads having to do with kitchen appliances, investment strategies, leisure holidays and the purchase of vehicles involves an almost exclusive proportion of mixed marriages. If we are to judge by frequency and repetition, we would have to conclude that such marriages outnumber by orders of magnitude any other nuptial arrangement. Indeed, it is rare to find a couple who are both white, as if these commercials implicitly endorse the canard of "white supremacy" or, as the title of a recent bestseller puts it, "white fragility," a paradigm that must be resisted. As Shelby Steele remarks in *White Guilt*, the current social zeitgeist focuses on a casuistical "manipulation of white guilt," a meme that is now widespread. White is aversive. It is no accident that when asked to generate images of people in all kinds of situations and contexts, Google Gemini's AI image generator prioritized diversity—black, brown, indigenous, female—but refused to portray white people. It is as if, in this case, the risible ads we are daily enduring were indirect adjuncts of Critical Race Theory.

That is how popular culture works today, surreptitiously infiltrating the popular mind with the usages, ideals, rituals and canons dear to the progressivist class. The violation of the norm, whether traditional or *even statistical*, the presenting a fiction as a fact, is the *modus operandi* of the budding totalitarian. Such is the scheme that the "hidden persuaders" of the current age have adopted.

As it should go without saying, there can be no objection to people's choice of goods and commodities, personal lifestyles, or partners and companions. Do as you will, provided it does no *material* harm or injury to others. Love or marry whomever you want, since marital success is determined by the compatibility of individuals and not by ideological complicities. But there is a strong objection to be made to the exercise of propaganda, whether overt or subtle, with the purpose of imposing a social and political agenda intended to subvert a long-standing and reasonably successful history and tradition—a tradition that underwrites and reinforces a prosperous nation and a viable way of life.

Many of today's ads, then, perform two tasks: they promote a product and at the same time insinuate a doctrinaire message. They reflect not merely consumer culture or the domestic world we have built at great cost over the centuries, but the world that the progressivist Left wishes to create and enforce—a world in which the founding peoples and their sustaining traditions, institutions and accomplishments will have been repressed and effectively eclipsed. A marriage between a man and a woman is no longer a universal standard. Children raised in same-sex unions are in no danger, apparently, of psychological disorientation. Women's sports are as qualitatively compelling as men's, though gate receipts show otherwise. The white race is a colonialist abomination and needs to be replaced or at least diluted. Such attitudes are taken for granted in the promotional milieu. None of this is stated. It is merely and incidentally suggested.

The personal response to this disinformative and tactical campaign is to consider the product but reject the message. A culture is built on criteria of unity and precedent. A democratic culture is built on the principle of freedom of thought, expression, assembly, religion and choice—and as should be obvious, the recognition of reality. But a culture that flies in the face of reality, that wilfully substitutes the heterodox for the normative, that practices affirmative action at the expense of truth, merit and a natural state of affairs will eventually collapse in rancor, misery, mediocrity and civil discord.

Advertising is carrying the water for a Leftist political and academic establishment. Its influence, because tacit, allusive, unspoken and only intimated, is perhaps the most effective means of persuasion of all—a telling illustration of "the extent to which the culture has been weaponized against us."

8
THE NEW LAGADIANS

Our intellectual classes today are utterly disconnected from reality. As Milo Yiannopoulos wrote in a review of the film *Joker*, "we are reeling from a disaster still unfolding, the unmaking of reality at the hands of millennial progressivism." Indeed, when it comes to unmaking reality, our cognitive elite may as well inhabit the parody world of *Gulliver's Travels*. Proposing blueprints for radical social change and meddling in the complexities of domestic and economic policy, they have come to resemble Jonathan Swift's pixilated "projectors" in the Academy of Lagado (Book 3, Chapter 5), a conclave of intellectuals and academics "full of volatile spirits acquired in that airy region" of vacuous irrationality.

In its effort to save the nation, Swift's Academy put forward various endeavors to advance the economy, improve education and become energy-self-sufficient. For example, it proposed "extracting sunbeams out of cucumbers, which were to be put in phials hermetically sealed, and let out to warm the air in raw inclement summers." This new technology "should be able to supply the governor's gardens with sunshine, at a reasonable rate." There was an astronomical plan "to place a sun-dial upon the great weathercock on the town-house, by adjusting the annual and diurnal motions of the earth and sun, so as to answer and coincide with all accidental turnings of the wind." Another project to improve land cultivation led to a Lysenko-like result, namely not a single ear of corn or blade of grass was to be seen. An ingenious "artist" set about employing spiders as weavers of silk, requiring an exhaustive effort grooming colored flies to feed the spiders, all to no purpose.

Nor should we forget the New Math of Swift's imagining, in which "[t]he proposition, and demonstration, were fairly written on a thin wafer, with ink composed of a cephalic tincture. This, the student was to swallow upon a fasting stomach, and for three days following, eat nothing but bread and water." The project was a failure since students regularly upchucked their educational diet. Another professor was "employed in a project for improving speculative knowledge," so that "the most ignorant person," by arbitrarily operating an "engine" made of bits of wood inscribed with letters, "might write books in philosophy, poetry, politics, laws, mathematics, and theology, without the least assistance from genius or study." A prominent landowner was tasked with using "wind and air" to run a mill, a work which miscarried miserably. As for architecture, the Academicians set about building houses by "beginning at the roof and working downward to the foundations." These new theories and practices had the predictable effect, leaving the country in a state of ruin.

As Gulliver's host explains to his bemused visitor: "In these colleges the professors contrive new rules and methods of agriculture and building, and new instruments, and tools for all trades and manufactures; whereby, as they undertake, one man shall do the work of ten; a palace may be built in a week, of materials so durable as to last for ever without repairing. All the fruits of the earth shall come to maturity at whatever season we think fit to choose, and increase a hundred fold more than they do at present; with innumerable other happy proposals. The only inconvenience is, that none of these projects are yet brought to perfection; and in the mean time, the whole country lies miserably waste, the houses in ruins, and the people without food or clothes."

Literary critics believe that the Academy of Lagado was conceived as a satire of the Royal Society, whose motto is *Nullius in verba*, often translated as "take nobody's word for it." Of course, Swift is not to be read literally since the object of his satire was not genuine science but the political and pseudo-scientific fashions of his day. The Society parses the tenor of its motto, adapted from the Roman poet Horace's *Epistles*, as "an expression of the determination of Fellows to withstand the domination of authority and to verify all statements by an appeal to facts determined by experiment." Swift would have concurred.

But in pursuing his satirical intent, which reads almost like a proleptic critique of postmodernism, Swift inadvertently foretold our "social democratic" and progressivist future as typified by the Democrat Party's "Green New Deal," among other pieces of lard-thick legislation. This project is designed to achieve net-zero carbon emissions; to convert 100 percent of power sources to renewable energy installations, thus replacing cheap, reliable energy with expensive, unreliable energy; to retrofit every building in the country in the interests of efficiency, at a cost destined to bankrupt the nation; to supplant air-travel with high-speed rail; to eliminate cows as methane infidels; and, among other vacant notions, to provide, in the words of pixilated Congresswoman Alexandria Ocasio-Cortez, "economic security for all those who are unable or unwilling to work"—with regard to the latter, a lifelong paid holiday exploiting a shrinking working class. The scheme is reminiscent of Nancy Pelosi's 2012 selling of Obamacare, which would allow Americans to quit their jobs and devote themselves to writing, music, photography or "whatever."

Rather, what is needed, as Don Watkins and Yaron Brook argue in their provocatively titled *Equality Is Unfair: America's Misguided Fight Against Income Inequality*, is to "liberate human ability," reanimate the fading concept of self-reliance, foster an ethos of industrious labor, and "liberate innovators from regulatory shackles" in order to "create a culture of achievement" and prevent the American dream from devolving into the American nightmare.

The Green New Deal is a crackpot enterprise that has enormous support from progressive economists and a staggeringly ignorant, partisan media. As economist Alan Carlin of The Heartland Institute wryly points out, "The program has been costed at a mere $93 trillion over ten years . . . This number may not mean much to most people, but it is roughly five times US gross national product" in that decade. Intellectual and economic bankruptcy, it would seem, are intimately allied.

Obviously, our New Lagadians are devoted members of the cultural Left, having made the long march through the institutions to radically reshape society in their utopian image. Rewriting the Royal Society motto, we might say that our "projectors" expect to be taken at their word, to have their authority submitted to, and to freely promote their theories and policy recommendations in the complete absence of "facts determined by experiment." Norman Rogers, author of *Dumb Energy: A Critique of Wind and Solar Energy*, has rigorously demonstrated the folly of the plan, "The Green New Deal is propped up by fake science and fake statistics," its research papers "masquerading as scientific studies." No matter. We are to take a conjuring trick as gospel truth.

Indeed, on the major issues of the historical moment—climate change, the war on terror, national borders, "social justice," gender politics, race conflict, Critical Race Theory, unrestrained immigration—the tribe of progressivist mountebanks wherever we find them gets everything wrong, opting for measures that only magnify the problems they affect to settle. We should not be surprised to find Lagadian absurdities in abundance, as for example: journeymen economists who advocate exorbitant spending to neutralize debt; politicians who endorse socialized medicine, at a cost of trillions and innumerable lives; senators who propose tax rates over 100 percent; teachers who believe that history is a narrative to be manipulated for ideological ends; leaders who champion near-unlimited Muslim refugee migration, generating communal strife, outright violence and unsustainable welfare expenditure; philosophers who affirm that truth is a relative concept—except for the truth of their own claims; revisionists who deplore the "mindless authority in European writing," with the exception of their own; agitators who promote violence as the road to millennial harmony; feminists who advocate the homicidal culling of men to create a better world; charlatans who claim that a cooling world gradually entering a new Little Ice Age is actually warming; the Bill Gates-AskeaBio plan to develop a vaccine to reduce livestock methane emissions, aka cow farts, to fight so-called "climate change"; medical practitioners who promote transgenderism and sex re-assignment surgery since the biological bodies we are born with are merely physical accessories; puritans who believe everything is about sex—excerpt sex; post-colonial theorists who claim that successful free-market societies are profiteering relics; geo-engineers who recommend shooting particles into the atmosphere to block the sun's presumably harmful rays; Luddites who want to selectively eliminate the fruits of technology and kill jobs; and so on.

Such quacks—Swift called them "speculators" and "virtuosi" —rely upon a mystical grimoire, a "book of shadows" filled with spells, incantations and rituals that will remake the world as if by magic. It's not science, it's enchantment. As Joshua Muravchik writes in *Heaven on Earth: The Rise, Fall, and Afterlife of Socialism*, the eclipse of historical memory of "the countless failures and abuses of socialism" ensures that the "old dream . . . retains the capacity to enchant." Orwell's observation in *Notes on Nationalism* that "One has to belong to the intelligentsia to believe things like that: no ordinary man could be such a fool" continues to apply. We are witnessing the Academy of Lagado on steroids.

Of course, the original Lagadians were not, technically speaking, socialists, they were fantasists pursing a collective delusion. But then, socialism is a fantasy no less destructive of social order and productive life than the Lagadian array of political and pseudo-scientific hallucinations, with which socialism bears a close affinity. To avoid descent into madness, reason must accommodate itself to reality. Sundered from the world as it is and divorced from nature, it generates only caricatures and deformities rather than solutions and pragmatic proposals for improvement. Having studied in the cloisters of our "woke" universities and relishing their epistemology of deceit, the New Lagadians turn the world upside-down and pretend that it is right-side-up. Having had the added benefit of reading Marx and Gramsci, and believing, as Justin Haskins writes in *Socialism Is Evil*, that "people will choose to behave in ways that seem contradictory to all human history and nature," they will not rest until they have succeeded in the "unmaking of reality," transforming a functioning economy and a great nation into an utter wasteland. They have, in effect, become proponents of what we may call transrealism.

For Haskins, socialism is not only economically but morally flawed since it ultimately entails collective coercion, that is, the imposition of stringent limits on diversity, individual liberty and freedom of worship. As for Gulliver, he may as well have been traveling in ruined and impoverished Venezuela, one of the great socialist miracles of our time. As he reports of his tour of Lagado, "The people in the streets walked fast, looked wild, their eyes fixed, and were generally in rags." The remainder of his journey "into several remote nations of the world" served only to deepen his misgivings and incredulity. The world about him suffers from a plague of moral disarray, mental stupefaction, technological madness and social disintegration, a kind of Gothan City writ large. He concludes his travels as a kind of Joker, unreconciled with his family, embittered by the prospect of a flawed and immoral society, and sinking into a state of misanthropy. Unlike Joker, however, he does not resort to mayhem, but gives himself over to dour solitude in rejection of a world that has betrayed common sense, reason and proper order.

Muravchik's vision of socialism is: "If you build it, they will leave." It seems more likely, given the millennial tenacity of Lagadian perversity as part of the socialist playbook, that one of two reactions will occur, either Joker's or Gulliver's, chaos or resignation. This is where we may shortly find ourselves.

9

THE CROUCHING
GOALTENDER

In the midst of the Stanley Cup finals, the thoughts of even serious people may turn to hockey. I make no claim to pundit-like seriousness, but I do confess to a love of the sport, and especially the craft of goaltending which has fascinated me since early childhood. Growing up in hockey-mad Quebec, I played on scrappy pick-up and local teams in preparation, so I hoped, for one day tending goal for the Montreal Canadiens, a team I idolized. It didn't work out that way, alas, but my interest in the game never flagged, and I still follow the careers and study the technique of the major NHL netminders.

One thing I've noticed is that, although individual goalies each have their unique styles, the collective mode of goaltending has changed dramatically. The heroes of my early youth were all stand-up goalies, occasionally with a slight shoulder-hitch—though sometimes, like Gerry McNeil of the Canadiens, they would go to one knee, the pose he favored on his hockey card. It looked rather classy. Nonetheless, they all pretty well stood their ground, or ice, for the most part vertically.

The greatest of them all was the Detroit Red Wings' Terry Sawchuk, whose like, I believe, has never been equaled. But they were all masters of the craft, and none wore masks (until Jacques

Plante of the Canadiens introduced the protective device). Harry Lumley of the Toronto Maple Leafs was a brick wall. Al Rollins of the perennially weak Chicago Black Hawks did, at times, resemble a sieve, but that was no fault of his own. If he'd had a strong defense in front of him, rather than the platoon of sad sacks who roamed the blue line instead of the deeper zone like a clutch of befuddled tourists, he might have achieved greatness. Sugar Jim Henry of the Boston Bruins, whose face looked like a puck-pummeled tattoo parlor, was an intimidating fixture between the pipes. No matter how many times he was stretchered off the ice, he would always return stronger than ever. At 5ft. 7in., Gump Worsely, shipped from the Rangers to the Canadiens, was a mighty mite. None were inclined to scrooch the ice or flop around, except when the situation demanded it.

Today's practitioners of the noble art are a different breed altogether. Their default position is the deep crouch, which makes some sense since most are a good half-foot taller than their predecessors and are able to cover a larger portion of the net. But the "top shelf" remains their weakness. I have rarely seen Jonathan Quick, formerly of the LA Kings—whose extraordinary reflexes, be it said, live up to his name—rise from his hams. Even the greatest goaltender of the current age, Andrei Vasilevskiy of the Tampa Bay Lightning, virtually impenetrable until recently, was perforated in the 2022 Cup finals by the Colorado Avalanche, who discovered an over-the-blocker weakness in his armor. If Vasilevskiy would have stayed upright, as did Sawchuk for the most part, he might scarcely have lost a game.

I don't mean to imply that there were not other stellar goaltenders who flourished in the more recent period: Plante himself, Glenn Hall, Ken Dryden, Billy Smith, Patrick Roy, Richard Brodeur, Carey Price, to name a few. But the earlier generation of stalwarts, playing with poorer equipment against fewer teams that could benefit from an obviously more rigorously selected and thus better talent pool of stickhandlers and sharpshooters, remain the giants of the profession.

I am baffled by this modern style of protecting the cage, shared by practically every netminder in the League. What has caused this paradigm shift? Why have goaltenders almost universally decided to "go down" or "hug the post" rather than follow the example of Terry Sawchuk and his tradecraft mates?

Of course, as noted, being taller and generally larger than their precursors, they blanket more of the net, but tending goal on one's knees has its, so to speak, downsides. There's a lot of slipping and sliding around, and the posture impedes the kinetics of defense, the ballet of anticipation. Primarily, it reduces what every goaltender depends on, what we might call "visionary scope," the ability to see the play developing, to recognize where the secondary shooters are, and where they are likely to reposition themselves. Standing tall helps to see through the "screen" intended "to take away his eyes,", as the sportscasters like to say. I'm not suggesting that the modern goalie never stands upright, but the trend toward crouching low to the ice is epidemic. And I don't get it.

If I were a poet, I'd be tempted to play with symbol and metaphor and say we are witnessing a sign of the times, however frivolous the notion. Are we as a culture returning to a more primitive stage of evolution? Is Homo Erectus now gradually sloping toward the drooping status of Homo Prolapsus, masked, padded, shielded, and though taller than our ancestors, somehow smaller than they were, less daring, less responsible, less willing to risk injury? Are we intent on seeking safety from the flying projectiles of the contemporary world, like those tiny viral pucks that a trucker-like Sugar Jim Henry would have no fear of and a citizen Terry Sawchuk would manfully deflect, relying on a natural immunity against being too easily scored on? We are not tending to our duty of spotting where the shooters are. So we stoop and bend and crouch and play it safe while the red light flashes behind us, like the worst goaltender ever to don the pads for *Les Canadiens*, the ineffable "Red Light" Racicot.

Mere speculation, of course, just having fun with the game of hockey and willing to play the game of life, to see through the screen that our adversaries have put before us, without crouching before the vicissitudes of existence and the mandates of the panic-mongers, as we are now prone to do. That, I propose, should be our goal.

10

IMPRISONED IN OUR CELL (PHONES): THE CURSE OF THE DIGITAL AGE

I'm sitting on a bench on the river boardwalk that skirts our quayside building, resting for a few minutes, sipping a coffee and taking my leisure after a pleasant saunter. I recall Thoreau's glorious passages in his essay *Walking* in which he stressed the importance of "sauntering," described as "the enterprise and adventure of the day." The word "saunter," he points out, derives from people "who roved about the country, in the Middle Ages, and asked charity, under pretense of going *a la Sainte Terre,* to the Holy Land, till the children exclaimed, 'There goes a Sainte-Terrer,'" in other words, a saunterer, a seeker capable of "sympathy with Intelligence."

Idly watching people walk by, I can't help noticing the ubiquitous prevalence of the cellphone, aka the smartphone, the constant companion of pedestrians everywhere. Just for the fun of it, I begin keeping score. Several individuals amble past, consulting their phones held like a wand or talisman in a raised arm. Then a couple, each with that obligatory device into which they stare with rapt attention, completely oblivious to one another. Next, a girl walking her dog, leash in one hand, cell in the other, followed a minute later by some fellow riding a bike, one hand on the handlebars, the other holding up a phone. Then, a young mother pushing a pram while intently reading the screen. Someone else walks by talking into plastic. A number of people are taking selfies. Clearly, one cannot saunter while wielding a cellphone.

Meanwhile, the scene around is alive with beauty and interest: flaming dogwood and Japanese cherry shedding their pink light into the air; plump koi speckled gold and cream gliding lazily in the ornamental pools and water gardens dotting the leafy esplanade; on the river, a tug hauling an immense freighter toward the docks and another towing a Seaspan chip barge to the sawmill, a loon preparing to dive and a seal or otter lifting its head from the waves. The tallest tin soldier in the world guards the entrance to the River Market, which seems to interest only children too young for cellphones. The largest sea gulls I have ever seen, some white, some gray, strut on a narrow sandbar. My friend Howard the Heron is busy deciding which of the logging bollards and pilings to perch on, his flight an act of pure grace. So much to look at! A passage from Walt Whitman's *Crossing Brooklyn Ferry* comes to mind:

> The sea-gulls oscillating their bodies, the hay-boat in the twilight . . .
> The scallop-edged waves in the twilight, the ladled cups, the frolicsome crests and glistening . . .
> the gray walls of the granite storehouses by the docks . . .
> the big steam-tug closely flank'd on each side by the barges . . .

But it is as if none of this exists—the extraordinary richness of ordinary experience drifting by unremarked. There is also the inner world of one's thoughts, memories and observations, which had always seemed to me more than sufficient to occupy one's waking, or walking, moments. Communing with oneself, one might learn that one is both an excellent conversationalist and a good listener. OK, kidding, but an inner landscape obliterated by the omnipresent cellphone is a melancholy thing to contemplate.

I recall some years back sharing a ride with a twenty-something girl in a car-dealership van on the way to pick up our newly inspected vehicles. She made no conversation with me or the driver, too absorbed in her screen, stroking it tenderly like a lover's cheek. Finally, I asked her, no doubt intrusively, why she paid so much attention to her cell. "Because I'm bored," she replied.

I was struck by her answer. After all, boredom has its upside. It can lead to a renewed appreciation of the sparkle of the world around one. It can force one to plumb one's inner resources. It can toughen one's resolve to see things through. It may provoke one to read a book. It's an anagram for bedroom. As Soren Kierkegaard put it in *Either/Or*, "Those who bore others are the plebeians, the crowd, the endless train of humanity in general; those who bore themselves are the chosen ones, the nobility," since they are the ones who are able to "entertain others." Boredom, said Adam Phillips in *On Kissing, Tickling and Being Bored*, "is akin to free-floating attention . . . Boredom is integral to the process of taking one's time." And, as French critic and semiotician Roland Barthes observed in a delightful collection of essays *Mythologies*, "Boredom is bliss viewed from the shores of pleasure." Indeed, figuring out Barthes' apothegm may also be a cure for boredom.

All these people I see walking by, eyes glued to the cellphone screen, trading trivialities with online friends, playing thumb-twiddling games, and surfing social media while the world is happening around them convince me that we are stumbling blindly into a new dark age. This is the future we are blithely welcoming. As James Bridle argues in *New Dark Age: Technology and the End of the Future*, "a kind of transport or transference [of information] is achieved, but at the same time a kind of disassociation, an offloading of . . . a way of thinking into a tool, where it no longer needs thinking to activate."

This is what Bridle calls a "chasm," a gap or crevice "that opens up between us when we fail to acknowledge and articulate present conditions . . . aspects of a new dark age that are real and immediate existential threats." Bridle is no Luddite and champions the proper use of our digital technology, which "depends upon attention to the here and now" and upon arriving at a symbiotic relation with our machines— "the things we think and discover together." He is concerned with avoiding "crashing ecosystems" and the like. His outlook remains positive, based on his belief that we "are not . . . without agency, and not limited by darkness." We are able to control our technological accomplices.

But it is hard to deny that the ecosystem governing thought, meaning and interpersonal relations is disintegrating. Something has been manifestly lost in our all-encompassing digital age—the free exchange of reflective minds, the habit of meditation, lateral awareness of the real world, and the very contours of the intro- spective and stable self. Libraries are growing obsolete— "in the age of Google and the iPhone," asks Michael Walsh in *The Fiery Angel*, "do we even need a 'library'?" We are swamped in a flood of information, most of it superficial and distracting, much of it false or misleading. We are constantly "connected" in a mammoth irony of disconnection from both self and other. A dystopian future we could once scarcely imagine may be coming to pass, a world no lon- ger confined to fiction.

Perhaps George Steiner was right when he imagined a future of small, monastic flares of intellectual light sprinkled across a des- olate landscape, reviving Max Weber's notion of frail enclaves of enlightenment as the last resort of a civilization sinking into dark- ness. I think, too, of Walter M. Miller Jr.'s classic *A Canticle for Lei- bowitz* with its obscure abbey in the Utah desert where historical knowledge is kept alive in a blighted world, even if it's only a sacred shopping list. The problem, as Barry Lopez says in *Arctic Dreams*, is that "The good minds still do not find each other often enough." Certainly not, especially if they, too, are wired to their cellphones.

In any event, the cellphone, for all its uses and convenience, is the bane of wakeful existence. To put it another way, the smartphone is not so smart. Italian detective story writer Andrea Camilleri has a striking passage in *The Safety Net*, in which his protagonist, Chief Inspector Salvo Montalbano, approaches a group of teenagers absorbed in their cellphones, locked in "their personal bubbles of isolation." Gazing at their faces, he sees that "all of them had pinpoint pupils and looked lost" and that none raised their heads to acknowledge him, "as would have been natural." He walks away, wondering how it was possible, "in the age of global communication, where all cultural, linguistic, geographical, and economic borders had been erased from the face of the earth, that this vast new realm had only created a multitude of loners, infinite numbers of lonely people in communication with one another, yes, but still in a state of utter solitude."

The cellphone, of course, is both an object and a symbol—a symbol of a far-flung network, as Bridle says, of "computational prediction, surveillance, ideology and representation" [that] inform[s] and shape[s] our present perceptions of reality." And that is the issue. For it is, in effect, precisely what it says, a "cell," in which we lock ourselves and throw away the key. The "phone" part is beside the point since we cannot take advantage of the one permitted call to a lawyer to arrange for our release—there is no lawyer in the cellphone world. "Stone walls do not a prison make," wrote poet Richard Lovelace in 1642, "Nor iron bars a cage." If the soul is free, he affirms, "minds innocent and quiet" may experience a "Hermitage" consecrated to the enjoyment of liberty. The same cannot be said for Gorilla Glass and a liquid crystal display, which is not a hermitage but a confinement whose parameters appear to be absolute.

Perhaps among the crowd of strollers, Brother Blacktooth, whom we first meet in Miller's sequel *Saint Leibowitz and the Wild Horse Woman*, bearing a staff instead of a cellphone, has embarked on an immense journey, a prolonged and adventurous saunter into the future and toward the distant light. The monk represents a ray of attenuated hope for the survival of intellect, discernment, thoughtfulness and what we used to call "spirit." But such a possibility is by no means clear. "A new world was rising," he notes, "but it could not grow as fast as the old." The new world he refers to is not the high-tech, solipsistic world we see around us but the world of a re-connected humanity pursuing its adventure of exploration and discovery. But Brother Blacktooth is right. It is not growing very fast.

11

DON'T YUCK MY YUM

Thou art sad; get thee a wife, get thee a wife!
– Shakespeare, *All's Well That Ends Well*

Let me say at the outset I'm not sure I'm qualified to write this chapter, having been married four times—though my wife Janice does not seem especially troubled, especially after I explained I was merely marrying my way to her. One might even say in my defense that I've had lots of practice and may actually have learned a thing or two about how to manage and survive this most profound of mysteries. I was encouraged to discover that my early philosophical hero Bertrand Russell also reveled in four wives. Multiple marriages may be construed as a protracted rite of passage.

I have often pondered my marriages, their ups and downs, their joys and miseries, their loyalties and betrayals, and in three instances, their melancholy break-ups. It's said that there are always two sides to a question, so it's often unclear who is responsible for a failed relationship. Though in my case I generally tend to endorse Jimmy Buffett's conclusion in *Margaritaville*: "It's my own damn fault." At least, I didn't pursue the Bluebeard option.

Among relatives, friends and acquaintances, scarcely a single union has remained intact, no doubt a feature of our morally fractured and narcissistic times, an age, we might say, of bed and circuses. Political and social frictions have also taken their toll in so vexed and querulous a culture as ours—a Republican married to a Democrat, a Trump supporter hitched to a Biden voter, a Covid skeptic paired with an avid jabber. All too often, I have seen such couples disintegrate or remain unhappily together for lack of a viable alternative.

It makes sense to recognize that sexual and romantic partners have a better chance of living happily together if they share a decisive number of basic ideas, habits, expectations and traditions, disagreeing only on minor matters or, when something more serious may arise, arriving at feasible ways of resolving disputes. In *12 Rules for Life*, Jordan Peterson explains that when he and his wife experienced a sometimes deep disagreement, "we would separate briefly, she to one room, me to another," where they would question the motives behind their irritation and anger. If the interrogation is honest, "then you can go back to your partner and reveal why you are an idiot."

Well, maybe. It usually takes me a day or two of simmering, a bottle of Scotch, and a terrible feeling of loneliness, before I can apologize or am ready to receive an apology. Luckily, such catering-to-self doesn't happen often. But it's a more natural if more painful way at arriving at a denouement, I believe. Peterson's is more clinical—but then, he's a professional psychologist. The great man once told me that if a couple agree on too many things, there could be problems ahead—a dictum I find passing strange. Many people, it must be said, just bury the issue that agitates them or damages the relationship, try to forget about it, and hope it doesn't emerge again. This is what I call a whack-a-mole marriage, and it never works.

What we call "open marriages" are generally, or should be, non-starters. They are rarely successful and, at least in my estimation and despite what the avant-garde may affirm, cannot kindle a genuine sense of intimacy and togetherness between two people. I had a friend, a well-known university prof, who arrived at such an arrangement with his wife. All went reasonably well for a time until his wife's paramour fell in love with her and created more trouble than he was worth. Meanwhile, my friend continued to indulge in his desultory affairs. His wife then took a second lover and my friend would come home to discover all manner of sex-related paraphernalia on the night table. He began to feel an intense discomfort and jealousy that, even when he put his liaisons behind him, continued to tear the marriage apart. This is only one instructive example among several I've been privy to.

I also know, both from literary history and personal experience, of marriages in which the men were unfaithful and the women not, as if indicative of what may be a biological fact, males spreading their seed and females preserving the blood line—a major motif in Shakespeare's plays. The great poet William Butler Yeats had an affair with a young poetess, which his wife Georgie Hyde-Lees did not object to and even encouraged—the poet was elderly and needed an inspirational boost, and he was, be it said, one of the cynosures of the Western canon. He deserved a little slack, apparently. Aldous Huxley's wife Maria procured for him, and the couple also enjoyed a long-lived threesome with Mary Hutchinson. Whether that makes the wife unfaithful is another question, since in the latter case she participates equally with her husband.

I'm not suggesting I recommend such practices, but despite the raging polemics of contemporary feminism or the disapproval of normal women, there is, admittedly, a patriarchal element in such indulgences which no amount of criticism and virulence will totally dispel. It seems part of the biological package. At the same time, women are no more exempt from such temptations, so it seems to be part of the "human package" as well. In any event, couples have to figure out these disruptions for themselves and find a strategy for taming nature rather than offloading their problems to some presumptive expert's guidance.

For I do not believe that marriage counselling is anything but a professional deception, as if marriage were an object with moving parts and a counsellor an ersatz mechanic whose expertise must inevitably lack projective inwardness and who may have an agenda of her own. (Such therapists are usually women, it seems.) A close friend of many years whose marriage was in shambles after he discovered his wife's infidelity agreed to consult a counsellor together with his partner. He noted that the specialist kept snapping pencils in two, the symbolism of which did not escape him.

He came to understand that the therapeutic impetus of modern culture was a vast and destructive illusion, eating away at personal agency and priapic self-assertion. He felt that the remedial mindset that pervades contemporary society produces the gradual erosion of personal integrity and moral accountability. Now re-married to a young and affable woman, he prefers the teaching of the Kabbalah, which proclaims that when a man and a woman unite in love and compatibility, an angel is born. This is another way of saying that one must find the right partner to keep the devil at bay.

For when it comes to the bridal choice a man may make, one thing is certain. Never wed a feminist. The original feminist may have been Adam's first wife, Lilith, who, according to the Old Testament Apocrypha was the mother of all evil and the womb from which all demons and vampires sprung. Unlike Eve she was created from mud and marl and her malign influence persists to the present day.

Clearly, when it comes to love and marriage, the complexity, the discrepant, even the incoherence seems unavoidable regardless of intention and good faith. Shakespeare begins one of his most well-known sonnets with the resonant phrase "Let me not to the marriage of true minds/Admit impediments; love is not love/ Which alters when it alteration finds." "True" means straight, but the poem develops the idea of "error," literally crookedness, wandering, bending, or infidelity. Even if one will be unfaithful—"though rosy lips and cheeks/Within his bending sickle's compass come"—the other will forgive and will not admit impediments. This is a tall order, plainly, and requires a certain heroic temperament not all of us possess.

Conservative thinker John Derbyshire addresses the same issue in his charming novel *Seeing Calvin Coolidge in a Dream*, which reads like a narrative gloss on Sonnet 116. He walks a fine line between error and truth, showing how forgiveness can lead to understanding and reconciliation, almost as if a marriage foundering on infidelity can be mended like a sort of *kintsugi*, the Japanese art of repairing broken vases with gold lacquer. But what goes for ceramics may not go for the more tortuous art of human relations.

One way or another, marriage is never a walk in the park, though it may have started that way. In the words of C.S. Lewis from *The Four Loves*, "Eros, having made his gigantic promise and shown you in glimpses what its performance would be like, has 'done his stuff.' He, like a godparent, makes the vows; it is we who must keep them. It is we who must labour to bring our daily life into even closer accordance with what the glimpses have revealed. *We must do the works of Eros when Eros is not present*." Those who idolize Eros will be sadly disappointed to find that marriage wasn't what they imagined it to be when the mundane routines of life rise to the surface replacing the excitement, the thrill, the ecstasy, the joy of the erotic and romantic beginnings of a marriage.

It's a prickly problem. What is to be done? Best, of course, to remain "true," if only after preliminary "error." To remain stoic if life becomes problematic. To follow the dictate of Paul in *Ephesians* 5: *So ought men to love their wives as their own bodies . . .* and the wife see that she reverence her husband. And it is important, as well, to be modest and playful and even a tad self-deprecating, as in Woody Allen's winsome quip: *Basically my wife was immature. I'd be at home in the bath and she'd come in and sink my boats.*

For a marriage to stay afloat, husband and wife must pledge not to sink one another's boats except in the bath.

12

REFLECTIONS OF A
PHILOSOPHY DROPOUT

One may review an actual situation by redescribing it
without making any mathematical or logical statement.
John Wisdom, *Paradox and Discovery*

I cannot put the subject through his paces in my inquiries
into his inclinations as I can in my inquiries into his
competences.
Gilbert Ryle, *The Concept of Mind*

As a student at the university, I intended to become a professional philosopher. I took my quota of graduate courses, learned to smoke a fisherman's pipe like the one cherished by my professor, and celebrated the great philosopher Immanuel Kant's birthday by drinking his favorite Médoc or Listán Blanco. (As Kant remarked in the *Critique of Judgement*, "Sparkling wine from the Canaries is very agreeable.") Puffing and quaffing led to intense speculations on the Transcendental Unity of Apperception and the Antinomies and Paralogisms. For Kant, the time needed for lighting and smoking his briar, as Manfred Kuehn pointed out in his fascinating biography, "was devoted to meditation."

The focus on wine and highfalutin meditation goes back to

Plato's *Symposium*. The pipe in particular is indelibly associated with the pursuit of wisdom. The cigarette belongs to the poet with his nervous, sporadic inspirations—say, Dylan Thomas—and the cigar to the novelist, the verbal tycoon, with his larger and more relaxed rhythms of composition—say, Thomas Mann. But the pipe is the philosopher's congenial instrument. The amount of time and fussing it requires to be kept lit furnishes the thinker with massive intervals of unrelated activity in which to formulate his abstruse and ineffable ideas.

This was especially true of Kantian studies where what might be benignly construed as a scholarly accessory assumed the status of a rigorous prerequisite. Our sessions over the *Critique of Pure Reason*, however, in which we tried to emulate our professor's Sobranie meditations, had the opposite effect on us. Smoke billowing from our intellectual chimneys, we coughed a lot and our eyes watered copiously in an enveloping atmosphere of fug and dottle. But we puffed heroically away as we gradually lost touch with the Paralogisms and saw the Axions of Intuition recede into the double obscurity of philosophical jargon and visual occlusion. We had obviously a long way to go to master the art of Transcendental scrutiny.

The seminar room presented another major problem. It had no windows. At the end of a three hour class on the Categories or the Dialectic the hallucinations came thick and fast and I would dash madly down the stairs, too desperate to wait for the elevator, just to reassure myself of the continued material existence of the ginko tree at the top of the campus. It was growing increasingly clear that although my grades were reasonably good my prospects were not, and that a philosophical career might be nothing more than a pipedream.

I attended courses in Ethics where we were taught to discriminate between the cash-value of practical conduct and the rubber cheque of theory. I was deeply impressed by my teacher in Greek philosophy, the kindly and diffident scion of a wealthy family, who had met Bertrand Russell— "good old Berty" as he called him—in his Yale days, discoursed endlessly on the Parmenidean dictum that *Whatever Is, Is*, and was chauffeured to class imposingly ensconced in the back seat of a big, green Bentley, like Plato sailing plutocratically into the court of Dionysus of Syracuse. And I was duly terrified by a lean, dry, inexorable Englishman who operated linguistically on such innocent statements as "Bismarck was an astute politician," disdained a priori concepts, and befuddled us with assertive links, ifs and cans, and illocutionary sentences.

Because the department was of the Analytic persuasion, it compensated for its bias with the occasional expensive French import. This was how the famous commentator on Sartre, Jean Wahl, found himself scurrying frantically between library and office, classroom and coffeehouse, always on the go, as if to present a moving target or stay out of the firing range of what must have appeared to him as a cavalry of jodhpur'd Positivists. As he was scarcely five feet high, the joke made the rounds that Jean Wahl had committed suicide by jumping off a curb.

The conflict that divided us in those days and set philosopher against philosopher in crusades of internecine pettiness was that between the British and Continental schools, a hangover from the English blockade of Napoleon. Empiricists and Existentialists could not bear to be in the same faculty lounge together. There was an apocryphal story that dramatized the absurdity of the dispute. At a prestigious conference on contemporary philosophy, a British Empiricist condemned the Continentals for vagueness of phrasing and hyperbolic imprecision of thought. "Tell him," said a leading French Existentialist on hearing of this piece of defamation, "that he is a cow."

The reason I did not take sides was that they were all equally bewildering: Kantians, Neo-Thomists, Positivists, Hegelians, Phenomenologists, Ordinary Language philosophers, the "whole sick crew," as Thomas Pynchon would say. To use the choice word of

Humpty Dumpty, the teetering founder of the school of Linguistic Analysis, they were of an unbreachable "impenetrability" —which meant, according to this learned arbiter, "We've had enough of that subject, and it would be just as well if you'd mention what you mean to do next, as I suppose you don't mean to stop here the rest of your life." Nevertheless, I persisted, deaf to good advice. Wittgenstein's *Tractatus* left me cold. I could not get past his paragraph numerology and agreed only with his conclusion, "What we cannot speak about we must pass over in silence," because that at least was understandable and because it coincided with Hamlet's dying speech. As for Husserl's *Ideas*, not a single word registered, and his *Cartesian Meditations* drove me to paroxysms of incomprehension.

Switching to Willard Quine was no antidote: identity, ostension and hypostasis made one feel as if one were developing cataracts. Heidegger's *Being and Time* was a disaster and I could see him only as the reverse counterpart of his namesake in Nathaniel Hawthorne's short story *Dr. Heidegger's Experiment:* Hawthorne's doctor possessed an elixir that made people younger but the torpid prose and tortuous thinking of the German philosopher aged me overnight. Clarence Lewis was better. The only problem with *Mind and the World-Order* was trying to divine why it had been written in the first place, as it seemed no more than the unfolding of a colossal tautology. Who had ever doubted that experience was such as to be amenable to conceptual formulation? Hegel's *Phenomenology of Spirit*, which I tried to breach three times, was no match for Tolkien's *The Lord of the Rings*, which served as both a replacement and a relief.

At one point I decided the only solution was to apply to the oracle himself. Accordingly, I sent off a letter to "Berty" who was living in Wales at the time, offering my services as amanuensis, occasional chess player and loyal apprentice. I described the turmoil and confusion generated by my studies and even confessed to a certain boredom, and that I preferred its anagram, "bedroom." Praising the titan for his indefatigable brainwork, his espousal of noble causes and his legendary excesses in the matrimonial field, I promised to be a good companion, a devoted student, and to let him win from time to time at chess. The letter concluded by congratulating the old man on his longevity but reminding him that even genius as it ages requires infusions of new blood, fresh perspectives and the intellectual buoyancy only youth can provide. The aging genius did not reply, an omission which looked at first like a personal insult and only afterwards as a critical appraisal of my philosophical ambitions.

As the semesters went by my faith began to waver with ever greater acuity. I was the only one in the class who thought that Samuel Johnson's refutation of Bishop Berkeley's principle of Subjective Idealism, namely, *esse est percipi* or to be is to be perceived, was basically sound. The perambulating doctor had kicked a curbstone and uttered the immortal words, "Thus I refute Bishop Berkeley."

One evening I visited the most brilliant student in the department who had devised a kind of Mercator projection of Hegel's *Phenomenology*. It was a road map of the Absolute, about one meter square, which resembled a cross between a genealogy table and the *Tibetan Book of the Dead*. Everything was neatly marked in black ink. All of Hegel, the whole labyrinthine country of that cluttered and tenebrous mind, lay spread out before me, while my benefactor performed miracles of explanatory acrobatics. When I left, I was more in the dark than ever.

The time had arrived to submit my thesis proposal to the department moguls. I had decided that what was missing in philosophy, as currently practiced and taught, was the sense of wonder and delight which had presumably informed its beginnings. Thus, I proposed a return to origins to which, as a student under the age of twenty, I was manifestly closer than my teachers, who were all over forty. Basing my intentions on the models of Parmenides and Lucretius who wrote in verse, I notified my advisors that I was ready to tackle the enigma of existence in all its primeval and crepuscular splendor and, moreover, would do so in decasyllabic metrics.

Instead of a prefatory Abstract, there would be an epigraph, suitably ambiguous, taken from Milton's *Il Penseroso*: "Where glowing embers through the room/Teach light to counterfeit a gloom." The stares of incredulity and affront which greeted this proposal served merely as a mild prelude to the storm of abuse that broke over my poor, unmortarboarded, anti-philosophical noggin. My betters were both stupefied and amazed. Philosophy, it seemed, not only began but ended in wonder. In the name of Wisdom, the presiding rota was incontinently Ryled.

Poetry, it must be remembered, operated as a rhetorical dismissive— "That's just poetry," the profs would sneer when crushing some notion or proposition advanced by their romantic catechumens. To address oneself not to the tidily articulated commonplaces of a celebrated British Analyst, preferably P.E. Strawson or A.J. Ayer, but to the richly inscrutable cosmic text authored by a nonentity and philosophical tyro like God, and to suggest verse as an appropriate medium for cognitive inquiry rather than the narrow and exclusionary technolect favored by a club of fastidious empiricists, was about as close as one could get to the kiss of academic death.

I was slowly coming to see that my philosophical career was in considerable jeopardy. Part of the trouble was that I had no Socratic *daimonion*, no inner voice that could always be counted on to tell one what *not* to do. If anything, I was possessed by its polar opposite, a contrary little devil out of Edgar Allen Poe, called the *Imp of the Perverse*, with a nasal twang egging me on to behave in ways precisely calculated to erect obstacles in my path, like proposing a thesis in verse on the prepreSocratics. Nevertheless, the temptation of secret gnosis continued irresistible.

I loathed the gnarled and idiosyncratic rhetoric of the German metaphysicians as I admired the ostensibly crisp and limpid prose of the 18th century Brits. The fact that I understood little of what they wrote did not deter me from seeking the invisible grail of wisdom that surely lay at the core of their testimony. And there was always the hope that one day I might experience the moment of visionary consummation, the noematic indescribable, the Kantian *ding an sich*, the Platonic *eidos*, the Aquinian music, in short, paydirt. My little impish voice said, "Go for it." And, credulous as always, I went for it, enduring yet another year of the Higher Bafflement.

Nothing offered to lighten my miseries, not even the occasional social encounter. I had made friends with a graduate student who intended to become a Neo-Kantian and we would regularly engage in long, pointless controversies over esoteric and insignificant questions, such as whether one could really generalize the maxim of one's conduct and whether one could do away with oneself if it violated the Categorical Imperative. Debating such deep and pressing issues, we found ourselves one evening at a Graduate Society party, smoking our pipes, wearing the obligatory tweed with leather elbows to complement the solemn expressions we assiduously cultivated, pretending to be oblivious to the fact that all the girls we secretly coveted seemed sublimely unaware of the charms of philosophical discourse and plainly preferred the company of sweet-talking literature majors and budding biochemists. Even the psychology and economics students were doing alright compared to us.

It came to me in a flash that "doing philosophy," as it was then called, was tantamount to committing eroticide, and that it didn't matter one bit if one could generalize the maxim of one's conduct or not because, whatever conclusion we arrived at, whatever triumph of intellectual insight graced our speculations, there could be no consolation for enforced celibacy. "The parchment philosopher has no traffic with the night," as Elizabeth Smart told us. One might as well take Holy Orders. The doubter was ripe for reality.

Trouble was, I had read my philosophers at least well enough to know that reality was a problematic concept, but this no longer appeared to matter very much. Whether reality could be proven by kicking a curbstone—the same curbstone, in a sense, that Jean Wahl jumped off—or by doubting everything but the Cartesian *cogito* that does the doubting or by bracketing empirical phenomena or by relying on *episteme* rather than *dianoia* to furnish a link with Truth or by catching a glimpse of the supersensual Forms and the *primum mobile* or by hitching a ride with World-Historical Reason on its way to Berlin, there was no point going it alone. This was like putting Descartes before the horse.

Condemning oneself to an existence without women was nothing short of suffering a terminal deprivation of the real Real. But even though I was by this time convinced that a man's true quest involved penetrating to the essence of muliebrity, aspiring to that condition which Ezra Pound in an early poem described as "after years of continence he hurled himself into a sea of six women," I had not yet succeeded in shrugging off a residual sense of guilt. Perhaps philosophy, like theology, subjected its candidates to harsh preliminary deficits in order to reward them at the end with the gold coin of knowledge and joy. Maybe the girls came later. Or failing that, a vision of ultimate clarity. Perhaps my thinking was still far too muddled to act upon. Should I wait just a little while longer before embarking on new ventures? Would lucidity finally arrive?

The *coup de grâce* was administered by two French professors on loan from the *Université de Montréal* who, riding in tandem, delivered a course on Existentialism and Phenomenology as part of their department's affectation of openness to a language other than French. To listen to the dual explication of Edmund Husserl in broken English and in process of constant mutual interruption was like falling under the simultaneous influence of alcohol and hashish—too drunk to see one's deliriums clearly. I retired early and did not attend another class for the rest of the term.

Learning that the final essay was due, I spent a weekend filling two examination booklets with my cogitations on philosophical luminaries Hams-Georg Gadamer and Wilhelm Dilthey, neither of whom I had ever read, in the gloriously turgid and sibylline language borrowed from Kant's *Prolegomena*. I was counting on the fact that the professors were as foreign to English as their student was to philosophy, but I did not expect more than a *soupçon* of Gallic amusement. *Quel divertissement!* I received the second highest grade in the course. And that did it. In a blaze of sudden enlightenment, I understood the truth about the philosophical fetish with reality; that is, "reality" was a dividend of not being found out, a credible simulation of what did not exist, a function of A.N. Prior's logical operator "Tonk"—the fudge factor that allowed whatever theory of the world you were brokering to work, a kind of "runabout inference ticket." In a word, one could argue that the cerebral fixation with "reality" was genuinely inauthentic, a prime example of philosophical cathexis. And since as a pseudo-philosopher I was already there, what would be the point in prolonging the redundant? So it was I abandoned the pursuit of the higher wisdom, free at last to indulge my natural laziness and duplicity in good conscience and become a poet. And, as always, richer in memories than in knowledge.

13
INSTAPOETRY: A SIGN OF CULTURAL DECLINE

The Distrest Poet, William Hogarth

L
ike sane political discourse, attentive reading and lucid
prose, poetry has fallen on hard times. Serious poetry
was always a highly specialized, aristocratic art (from
Greek ἀριστεία:aristeia, "excellence," "nobility,"), something rarefied and patrician. That is why indiscriminate profusion is a bad
sign. By my, albeit whimsical, estimation, in Canada alone there are
at least two poets per capita. In America, one need only consult The
Poetry Foundation to find an innumerable cohort of poetic nonentities who have brought the craft down to the level of barstool
confessions, thanks in large measure to the pedestrian influence of

Robert Lowell's *Life Studies* with its all-too-intimate revelations of self, its reminiscences of personal trials and ordeals, its family histories, and its flat, prosaic, unbosoming language—a paradigm going back to Wordsworth's inaugural *The Prelude*. (Though Wordsworth accomplished the feat with genius.) As a result, poetry on the whole seems to have become mainly kibbitz, mere undistinguished palaver, a token of egalitarian self-promotion. "Shouldn't it be possible," asks David Orr in *Beautiful and Pointless*, "for us to read poems without thinking of 'the personal' at all?"

The baleful effects of the impulse toward self-disclosure, chat and vent are visibly prominent in the office of our national Laureateships. The installation of Canada's current Parliamentary Poet Laureate Georgette LeBlanc, for example, is primarily a nod to the "French fact," a political move that has nothing to do with poetic excellence. Her poems are adiabatic, neither bad nor good, consisting mainly of reminiscence and a kind of domestic commentary. The American incumbent at the time Joy Harjo relies on her indigenous status to regale us with tedious narratives of personal trauma and collective suffering. These laurel offerings are ™poems, autobiographical and therapeutic in nature, "placing inadequacy," as Christopher Grobe writes in *The Art of Confession*, "where we expected an epiphany." The prestige of such poetry is ubiquitous. And if this were not bad enough, the situation has now deteriorated, possibly beyond recovery, owing to the easy access and uncritical circulation afforded by the Internet.

Typified by the absence of intellectual integrity and serious craftsmanship, a new species of poetic writing, known as InstaPoetry, has emerged and is now flooding the mediascape. It represents what Frank Furedi in *The Power of Reading* calls the "decoupling of literature from cultural content [and from] the exercise of judgement." By "cultural content," Furedi is not alluding only to the cultural philistinism of the moment but means something like Matthew Arnold's "the best which has been thought and said in the world" and "the study of perfection." Stemming in part from a "fetishized orientation toward the mass impact" of technology and new media which have devastated the cognitive landscape, Furedi's "decoupling" is an index of the intellectual vagrancy and bad faith, abetted by the open sluices of the Internet, that epitomize an increasingly degenerate culture and its poetic output.

Similarly, as Adam Garfinkle argues in *National Affairs*, "cognitively sped-up and multitasking young brains may not acquire sufficient capacities for critical thinking, personal reflection, imagination, and empathy"—qualities necessary for what Maryanne Wolf in *Reader, Come Home*, cited by Garfinkle, calls "deep literacy," a capacity that reflects reading and writing "with the potential to bear original insight."

Given the decline in cognitive capacity that Furedi, Garfinkle, Wolf and others lament, it is no surprise to find Rumaan Alam at *The New Republic* consecrating Canada's Insta sensation Rupi Kaur as "Writer of the Decade." Kaur, with a degree in Rhetoric and Professional Writing from the University of Waterloo, has sold millions of copies of episodic natterings. Her sappy, infantile maunderings not only sound the death knell of real poetry but serve as an illustration of what the Internet has done to the sad remnants of popular taste. According to Alam, Kaur "understands better than most of her contemporaries how future generations will read." That, I submit, is the problem.

It may also be how future generations will write. As the great critic Hugh Kenner bemoans in *Gnomon*, "we observe, among other symptoms, a student population so illiterate it cannot read poetry at all." Composition is equally moot. Here is a typical Rupi Kaur poem from the sun and her flowers:

> like the rainbow
> after the rain
> joy will reveal itself
> after sorrow

Obviously, there is nothing much there. The insight is trivial. Cadence is non-existent. The metaphor of the rainbow is an unadorned cliché that remains undeveloped in some unanticipated way that might rescue it from utter banality—for example, as in Bobby Borchers' singable "Promised Her a Rainbow" with the clever refrain: "I promised her a rainbow/and gave her the rain." The Rolling Stones can get away with the platitude in their hit song "She's a Rainbow", thanks to the musical accompaniment: vocals, instrumentation and melody that embellish the trope. But poetry requires precision and originality, as well as the capacity to create a ripple effect in the mind—in short, an architectonic. Think of Emily Dickinson's stanza with its Worsworthian conclusion:

> The rainbow never tells me
> That gust and storm are by,
> Yet is she more convincing
> Than Philosophy.

Or Australian poet Les Murray's "An Absolutely Ordinary Rainbow" about a man weeping in the street and the crowd who

> feel, with amazement, their minds
> longing for tears as children for a rainbow.

Or William Wordsworth's figural rainbow template in "My Heart Leaps Up," echoing the *Book of Genesis*.

Instagram poets are a coterie of pretty dull blades who think they are cutting edge. They are certainly not "distrest," like Hogarth's garrett-bound scribbler. Reviewing another Canadian, the masked Instapoet code-named Atticus who read last year at the Strand bookstore in New York, William Logan writing in *The New Criterion* is almost affronted. "There's scarcely a metaphor in the book that isn't a cliché shoplifted from Walmart," Logan muses in disbelief. What is one to make of these approximate ten-liners filled with "cotton-candy sentiment and malignant drivel, which show no more intelligence than a fried potato?" Harsh words but true. At the New York reading, Atticus expressed the hope that his work and social media presence would be "a gateway drug to classical literature." As he told *The Globe and Mail*, Atticus feels fortunate to have taken poetry classes at Wadham College at the University of Oxford, which might explain the sentiment. Here is a typical Atticus poem from *The Truth about Magic*:

> "I don't know many things
> with any certainty,"
> she said
> "but snuggling feels important."

One can see the problem with this snippet: its absolute triteness and its encapsulation entirely within itself, qualities that blanket his entire production. What we are observing is the dreck effect in action. One might say that that "deep reading" is beside the point here since, as Wolf writes, "all deep reading requires the use of analogical reasoning and inference if we are to uncover the multiple layers of meaning in what we read." *There are no multiple layers of meaning in Instapoetry.*

In a comprehensive article *Instagram Poetry Is A Huckster's Paradise* in the *Huffington Post*, Claire Fallon points out that Instagram poetry is an industry and its practitioners are "brands" —actually, this is Atticus' word from *The Globe and Mail* interview—whose "appearances cohere into a marketable aesthetic" and whose verses, "in their conceptual simplicity and linguistic timidity read like parodies of poetic schmaltz." The genre, however, remains hugely popular because "for these Instagram poets and their audiences, creating fresh, original verse isn't the point." Instead, the traditional gatekeeper system is down in order to welcome marginalized voices, "purveyors of female empowerment and romantic expression," as well as "scammers and opportunists and ironists faking sincerity" — and, as she points out, plagiarists, too. Fallon's critique is persuasive, especially as she writes from a doctrinaire alt-left perspective native to the HuffPo where a greater sympathy for these tender-minded millennials might have been expected.

That millions of people are buying Instagram poetry does not change the fact that it is self-indulgent rubbish aimed at an unevolved readership unlikely to graduate to the works of the classics from the Greeks to the Victorians, or of the great "modern" poets like Emily Dickinson, Walt Whitman, Gerard Manley Hopkins, Robert Frost, Daryl Hine, Richard Wilbur, Seamus Heaney, James Merrill, Philip Larkin and Irving Layton, or living poets of accomplishment like Peter Van Toorn, Kei Miller, Eric Ormsby and Bill Coyle.

Many readers and writers, especially of the millennial set, will claim that I'm speaking down, a snobbish relic of an earlier generation. I suppose that the same would need to be said of Camille Paglia who, in *Break, Blow, Burn*, mourns the virtual extinction of lyric poetry, "which from its birth in ancient Greece has played so significant a role in the emergence of individualism, spawning in turn our concept of civil rights." We have, she regrets, forfeited "custodianship" to "deconstruction" —and to the inability to defer gratification, the unwillingness, let's say, to steal time from sleep.

True poetry lovers and real poets are at a discount these days, made to feel irrelevant and superannuated, if not apologetic. A jesting remark of Sir Walter Raleigh's comes to mind: "If I am accused on Judgement Day of teaching literature, I shall plead that I never believed in it and that I maintained a wife and children." All I can say in response is that if you do not know, or strive to know, the history of your culture, nation and civilization; if you have not learned, or have not tried to learn, the grammatical rules, expressive possibilities and rhetorical cadences of your language, especially if you harbor literary aspirations; if you refuse to submit to a long and arduous apprenticeship in your chosen craft, including a familiarity with its formative tradition that serves as the basis for poetic innovation; and, in short, if you have not "read deeply," as Maryanne Wolf urges, then it follows that your thought processes will remain larval and your practice vain and superficial, regardless of your age and current enthusiasms.

Indeed, it should go without saying that without a thorough grounding in what came before and an internalizations of the technical aspects of the art, a poet cannot expect to produce much that is not ephemeral. After all, if you wish to excel, you have to know your stuff. Bill Coyle's intricate yet colloquial sestina with its six rotating rhymes across six stanzas and a triplet coda, "Abandoned Bridges" from *The God of This World to His Prophet*, says it clearly, both in illustration and theme:

> For now you fathom how those bridges,
> as needful as they were before,
> only grow more so over time,
> how they lead us to a past
> inaccessible by roads.
> You look toward the other side.

Alam approves of a poetry that works "within the parameters of a smartphone screen" —a sign, I suspect, of limited attention span and dwindling focus. To write poetry that speaks of the dilemma of consciousness in a world of mortality, that plumbs the mysteries of the human heart, that responds with satiric exuberance, manifest eloquence or heart-rending directness to the complexities of experience, that drives for beauty rather than "pleasure technology," as poet Dana Gioia puts it in his well-known talk *Why Beauty Matters*, and that embeds its wisdom in the memorable line or phrase or verse that stays with us—well, a smartphone screen just won't do.

I would suggest to any Internet practitioner serious about his or her craft—there may be one or two, though I have yet to find them—to junk the smartphone and the media platforms and get down to the real business of poetry by consulting what won't fit on a screen or an Instagram post. For example: an epic scroll, like James Merrill's magisterial *The Changing Light at Sandover* or Michael Lind's masterpiece in rhyme royal The *Alamo*; or a crown of sonnets, like David Trinidad's "A Poet's Death" in *The Late Show*; or Paul Muldoon's *"Encheiresin Naturae"* in *Frolic and Detour*. Muldoon writes a "Heroic Crown," in which a fifteenth sonnet deftly reprises the lines of the previous fourteen. The title is an alchemical allusion to the "Spirit of the Earth" in Goethe's *Faust* and the bonding of spirit and flesh in William Butler Yeats' *Supernatural Songs,* providing the kind of rich amalgam of the literary, historical and personal dimensions utterly foreign to the kitsch and mummy wheat of the Instagram mind. (That many of Muldoon's poems hew rather snidely to the left and are ruined by partisan boilerplate does not alter the fact that, in this case, a good poem is a good poem.)

Perhaps our Instapoets might learn the rugosities of the art they profess by working occasionally in strict verse forms such as the villanelle, consisting of five tercets with alternating first and third rhyming lines, which then comprise the final couplet of a concluding quatrain. Among the most beautiful such exemplars in the language are Dylan Thomas' "Do Not Go Gentle," Elizabeth Bishop's "One Art" and Robyn Sarah's "Villanelle for a Cool April," which can serve as models for emulation. Or they might aim for the long haul, say something like Alice Oswald's fascinating and protean variation on the *Odyssey*, *Nobody*, whose gorgeous syntactical "waves pass each other from one colour to the next," and which demands both prior knowledge and dogged stick-to-it-iveness. Of course, these virtues are no guarantee of excellence, but they at least give the poet a chance at it. Such application would constitute a valuable learning experience and would certainly enhance the quality of concentration in a media-distracted world.

Distraction, along with short attention spans, is the root of the problem. How, asks Maggie Johnson in *Distracted: Reclaiming Our Focus in a World of Lost Attention* can we turn "epidemic distraction into exquisitely engaged minds?" How to create a "renaissance of attention . . . in a distractible world" is the pivotal issue, she suggests, if we are to build and inhabit an "ambient presence" and a culture of patience in order to produce anything of value. No easy answer. But we must somehow recover, she stresses, "the ability to pause, focus, connect, judge and enter deeply into a relationship or an idea," which takes logarithmic time and sustained attention.

Johnson mentions the painter Anthony Ryder, "who spends up to seventy hours on a single drawing." I recall my colleague Peter Van Toorn who would accumulate a hundred drafts for a single line of poetry, as evident in the verve and polish of his classic volume *Mountain Tea*, one of the finest collections to appear in the Canadian poetic muniment. The alternative, as we see in Instapoetry, is a "numb[ness] of easy diffusion" and nervous recoil from the reign of artistry, or in the words of Robbie Burns from "Address to a Haggis": It's the sort of "olio to staw a sow or fricasee wad mak her spew wi' perfect sconner!" Johnson remains hopeful that a cultural reset is possible but, apart from individual exceptions like those I have mentioned, I am not so sanguine.

In *Politics and the English Language*, George Orwell argued that language is becoming "worn out," "unevocative," "vague," "abstract," "prefabricated," "stupid" and "sentimental," and that "our thoughts are foolish." Had he only seen the effect of the Internet on thought and language he would be spinning in his grave like a pulsar. The practice of Instagram poetry constitutes only the latest proof of Orwell's grim assessment. Minds untrained in the rigors of the discipline they avow and fascinated by the epicurean ease of digital composition-and-distribution can generate little but callow observations and pretentious commonplaces best harbored in private. That such work has achieved public success is a testament to the soporific dullness that has overtaken us.

"[P]oetry makes nothing happen," wrote W.H. Auden in his moving elegy for W.B. Yeats; it survives only in "the valley of its making." But poetry may still be useful in that it serves, if not as a remedy, certainly as a symptom of the current state of the culture. It helps us read the etiological chart. In declining times, all that serious poets can do, whether "distrest" or not, as the Koholet advised in *Ecclesiastes* 9:10, is find the work they must do with their hands and do it with their might, rather than indulge the jubilant plunge into untutored sentiment, unadulterated emotionalism and mere chatter.

To quote my former correspondent and revered mentor the late Richard Wilbur, who put it succinctly in a brilliant lyric titled "Ceremony," "Ho Hum. I am for wit and wakefulness." Can't argue with that.

14
GIORGIO DE CHIRICO
AND COVID-19

The Enigma of an Autumn Afternoon, (1924)

The city, for all its anonymity, traffic congestion and claustrophobic density, is the center of the economic and cultural life of a people. What happens to the city happens to the nation and ultimately to the character of its citizens. British philosopher John Gray in his aphoristic tract on humanistic folly *Straw Dogs* is of a different mind, speaking of the grand delusion of stability represented by great cities, especially in the modern era. He observes that "In cities, persons are shadows of places . . . The settled life they once contained is fading from memory." Images of our cities in the wake of draconian COVID legislation emphasize the point.

Giorgio de Chirico (1888-1978) is considered by many as one

of the signature painters of cities in the tradition of Western art, as, for example, Canalleto was famous for his views of Venice and its canals. But de Chirico's paintings were not merely representational; in the words of French poet Guillaume Apollinaire, they were best described as a kind of "Metaphysical Painting," relying on a technique of disorientation to develop a perspective on reality hidden by our habitual preoccupations and assumptions about the world, and to enact in paint a revelation of the guileful and enigmatic nature of consensual experience that glazes over the primal strangeness of the world and the natal loneliness of being:

The Enigma of a Day, (1914)

De Chirico's canvasses "read" like a synthesis of riddle and parable. "One must imagine everything in the world to be a riddle," he wrote in *Memoirs*. His imaginary cityscapes, empty plazas, long arcades, brooding figures and sculptural fragments are ways of making us confront what he liked to call, in work after work, the "enigma" underlying everything we see and do, all that normal perception and belief tend to suppress or overlay with facsimiles of "the real." His intention was to expose the distortions and distractions that consciousness provides for our solace and comfort in a world that neither loves nor needs us. Horror author and cult figure Thomas Ligotti might well have had de Chirico in mind when he wrote, in *The Conspiracy against the Human Race*, that we are invested in immunizing awareness "from any thoughts that are startling and dreadful" in order to perpetuate a "falsifying and specious view of ourselves."

A de Chirico painting repays contemplation for its bizarre motifs and eerie insights into and beneath the surface of the world we take for granted. But the world of de Chirico's phosphorescent imagination— "phosphorescent" is his word—brings to mind a twisted aspect of presentational immediacy. His spectral cityscapes now suggest the agenda of our political leaders who led us into a caricature of de Chirico's art, a travesty which is also worth contemplating, but only as a function of disembrained planning. They are not visionaries but curators of disaster, embodied shadows cast by the totalitarian architecture of deceit and stupidity. The destabilization of practical life caused by the official response of masks, quarantines, lockdowns, experimental vaccines and endlessly evolving mandates to the COVID panic and variant obsession turned our cities into ghost conurbations and deep-sixed the economy of nations into the bargain. Some scholars believe it may take a decade to return to the former status quo, others say a generation, Klaus Schwab of the World Economic Forum says "never." He may be right. Certainly, our cities, that featured shuttered shops, half-vacant office towers, phantom skyscrapers, half-deserted lanes and by-ways, and sparsely populated parks, will never quite be the same again—an aura of desolation fortuitously captured in de Chirico's *The Enigma of Skyscraper.*

In *Metaphysics of Silence: Giorgio De Chirico,* Lucio Giuliodori's summation of the impression left by certain paintings casts a premonitory light on the pandemic practices of our political gauleiters, mired "in the throes of a kind of dehumanizing effect . . . in a world ruled by madness rather than rationality." Of course, the Pictor Optimus (as he is known to his admirers) wasn't thinking of political contingencies, plagues or natural disasters, but of the metaphysical quality of deep perception, of the reality of sadness, menace, dislocation and emptiness beneath the laminate of ordinary life and the consoling illusion of common expectation. Yet, as art critic Maximiliano Duran has pointed out, our cities under lockdown were weird, serendipitous projections of de Chirico's strange and unsettling vision. He quotes a colleague who wrote at the time: "When we walk in Turin today, it is as if we are walking inside a de Chirico." The phrase was picked up in a video essay by Evan Puschak (aka The Nerdwriter), worth seeking out.

De Chirico's art is plainly "metaphysical" in Apollonaire's sense— "meta" is the Greek prefix for "after" or "beyond" — thus beyond the physical. (Giuliodori puts it somewhat differently, though to the same effect: "He didn't set metaphysics beyond physics but rather in physics, deep into the hidden core of it.") The "art" of our political leaders and their medical cronies, however, was and is anything but metaphysical or even intelligent; rather, not only misguided but punitive and spiteful, a mutilation of the physical. They succeeded in turning de Chirico's mysterious mises-en-scène and avowedly melancholic deconstructions of the customary into grim empirical realities, embarking on a program that not only failed but caused unparalleled devastation.

The havoc they released in following the prescriptions of a self-interested medical profession is unprecedented in peacetime, rupturing the social fabric, wrecking the economic life of entire countries and emptying our city streets and buildings of activity, commerce and pleasure. A visit by our ostensible superiors to the Tate or MoMa or Palazzo Strozzi, where de Chirico's oeuvre has been on exhibit, would have been far more beneficial than consulting Anthony Fauci or Neil Ferguson, corrupt and incompetent "experts" who got everything wrong, or relying on their own timorous and mediocre judgment. They created not a work of imagination but a palpable monstrosity.

One recalls Joseph Conrad's famous statement of purpose: "My task is . . . before all, to make you see." The visions of great artists and writers will often have predictive value, but not always as strict reproductions of the everyday world. They will occasionally assume ironic and unexpected manifestations, semantic fictions or visual exaggerations that become uncannily prescient and part of the sediment of actual existence, like Kafka's deformed and irrational judicial system in *The Trial.* In such cases, irrealism tends to become fact, and implausibility, truth. Today, making allowance for the distinction between acumen and stupefaction, the painter and the politician, we are indeed walking in a de Chirico.

The Enigma of the Hour, (1911)

15

IN PRAISE OF CARBON

The demonization of carbon, the very basis of all life on earth, can only be explained as a sacrilege and a perversity.
— John Brignell

In an op-ed in *The New York Post*, "Don't buy the latest climate-change alarmism," "climate skeptic" Bjorn Lomborg, accepts that the earth is indeed gradually warming. This does not prevent him from arguing that the frenzy regarding the immediate or long-term heating of the atmosphere, owing to what we might call "carbon load," and the specter of terrestrial catastrophe accompanying it, are utterly misplaced. We are emphatically not in the midst of the climate cataclysm that Global Warmists insist is impending.

Lomborg's *The Skeptical Environmentalist* (2001) and *Cool It* (2010) advance to a considerable extent an economic rather than a purely scientific argument. His most recent book *False Alarm* (2020) by no means eschews the economic factor but focuses on the dodgy science and apocalyptic fever that are currently agitating a portion of the scientific community and roiling public consciousness.

Global warming mitigation strategies are chiefly about power, wealth, reputation, research grants and professional sinecures. They are about the Leftist agenda to replace a free-market economy with a command economy. Those who endorse the hurricane of dooms-day warnings, repeated every few years despite the evident lack of ecological compliance, do not have the time of day for Lomborg except to excoriate him.

In the *NYP* op-ed, Lomborg agrees with the UN's IPCC report that global warming is a serious problem, but deplores "how much one-sided thinking takes place in the climate conversation." The report "confirms that climate change indeed has increased heatwaves." However, without dwelling on the subject, "the report tells us that global warming means the frequency and intensity of cold extremes have decreased."

Lomborg continues: "This matters because globally, many more people die from cold than from heat. A new study in the high-ly respected journal *The Lancet* shows that about half a million peo-ple die from heat per year, but 4.5 million people die from cold." To its credit, the IPCC report also mentions in passing "that more CO_2 in the atmosphere has acted as a fertilizer and created a pro-found global greening of the planet. One NASA study found that over a period of 35 years, climate change has added an area of green equivalent to twice the size of the continental United States. But don't expect to read about this in any of the breathless articles on climate impact."

Lomborg's brief is supported by Michael Shellenberger's au-thoritative *Apocalypse Never* (2020) and was anticipated by Robert Zubrin, whose *Merchants of Despair* (2013) effectively laid out the case for the miracle and necessity of a rich lading of environmen-tal CO2—a counterintuitive fact not understood by the blinkered catastrophism of the global warming crowd. No carbon, no food. Less carbon, less food. The war against carbon boils down—no pun intended—to a war against human flourishing. As Zubrin puts it, the theory of harmful global warming "is the core idea of anti-humanism," of which the once noble idea of environmentalism has become a chief incubator.

Zubrin points out that there exists robust scientific proof derived from ice core data and isotopic ratios in marine organism remains that Earth's climate is ultimately a *stable system*, that CO_2 emissions create surplus plant growth that in turn absorbs any untoward excess of atmospheric carbon dioxide, thus restoring climate equilibrium over the long term, and that under conditions of cyclical global warming agricultural productivity naturally increases for the benefit of humanity. Warmth and nourishment are certainly to be preferred to cold and scarcity.

Indeed, as the *Advanced Material, Processes and Energy Devices* program at the University of Arizona explains, "All life on planet earth is bound by one common factor: carbon." That is, biomolecules like proteins, DNA, and carbohydrates are all carbon-based molecules. Reducing carbon imperils plant and animal life and consequently human life as well. The concentration of CO_2 in the atmosphere is just .04%. The fact is, we need more of it, not less.

Similarly, the Heartland Institute (December 20, 2024) has assembled a considerable number of premier studies and science papers providing conclusive evidence that most man-made CO_2 has always been quickly absorbed in the biosphere—"which leads to substantial, famine-busting plant growth. The remaining CO_2 enters a saturated atmosphere and has a minimal effect on global temperatures . . . This means little or no further warming is to be expected, and that rising atmospheric CO_2 levels are 100% beneficial." Of course, none of this information "will be reported in the media since it disrupts the hysterical climate science narrative tied to their regular doom-laden apocalyptic predictions, and the insanely destructive 'Net Zero' fantasy.

Extensive scientific research conducted by the Fraser Institute and reported in its 1997 publication *Global Warming: The Science and the Politics* reminds us that CO_2 levels during the Ordovician Age 440 million years ago were ten times higher than they are at present.

Writing in the *Wall Street Journal* (March 27, 2012), acclaimed Princeton physicist William Happer also highlights the fact that "Life on earth flourished for hundreds of million years at much higher CO_2 levels than we see today."

Happer's *"The Truth About Greenhouse Gasses"* in *First Things* (July/August 2011) presents the facts. "As far as green plants are concerned," he writes, "CO_2 is not a pollutant, but part of their daily bread . . . Most green plants evolved at CO_2 levels of several thousand ppm [parts per million], many times higher than now. Plants grow better and have better flowers and fruit at higher levels. Commercial greenhouse operators recognize this when they artificially increase the concentrations inside their greenhouses to over 1000 ppm." He points out that "the Navy recommends an upper limit of about 8000 ppm for [submarine] cruises of ninety days, and NASA recommends an upper limit of 5000 ppm for missions of one thousand days. We conclude that atmospheric CO_2 levels should be above 150 ppm to avoid harming green plants and below about 5000 ppm to avoid harming people." *The current level is approximately 400 ppm.*

Zubrin's and Happer's analyses are a welcome counterpoise to Lomberg's partial naivety concerning global warming. Still, Lomborg's circumspectly compatible handling of the IPCC's 4000 page "code red for humanity" assessment was not entirely unexpected. He is critical of some aspects of it, less so of others. But the unvarnished truth of the matter is that the various techniques and interventions employed by the Green industry to reduce our so-called "carbon footprint" —carbon capture, carbon offsets (a complete canard), electric vehicles (so to speak, a non-starter), a landscape-despoiling architecture of wind turbines and solar panels—are not only largely unworkable and punitively costly but are actually counter-productive. Neither the economy nor the electrical grid can sustain them, and neither can our supermarket shelves. The planet is not only not going to burn up or sink beneath the seas; rather, if climate projections from the best authorities are disregarded, it may freeze before its time.

For it appears that we are entering a Solar Minimum when the solar magnetic field diminishes and cosmic radiation increases, producing greater cloud cover and eventually cooler temperatures. Agricultural and environmental economist Donald Avery furnishes the latest data from the CERN particle physics lab, which "foresees no runaway warming. Instead, it sees an impending cold solar minimum." Further corroboration comes from many reputable sources, including Anrab Rai Choudhuri's closely reasoned *Nature's Third Cycle* (2015). Choudhuri yields supporting evidence for drastically reduced sunspot activity and the prospect of cooling summers and harsh winters to come. We are in the initial stages of this development now.

Naturally, there will be heatwaves, which Warmists will seize upon to justify their prepossession; the inevitable cold spells will be dismissed and forgotten since these are unwelcome intervals of climatological refutation, or treated as events to be data-manipulated to suggest the opposite. *The New York Times* (2008), for example, quoted an array of scientists who regard cooling events as merely "a cold kick from the tropical Pacific Ocean." Nothing much to see here. After all, "Many scientists also say that the cool spell in no way undermines the enormous body of evidence pointing to a warming world." Cold periods, then, are temporary fluctuations in weather patterns, nothing more, according to the doofus reading of climate data.

A NASA bulletin (2010) added its weight to the hypothesis. A pressure pattern called the Arctic Oscillation can cause "unseasonably cold air masses to sweep over what are normally temperate latitudes," a local or interim phenomenon. Cold spells then become indisputable signs of a planet heating up. The effect is presumably abetted by a mechanism called "radiative forcing," a chemical chain reaction producing a multiplier heat result affecting the earth's energy budget. You can't win. Present cold equals future hot. Even if humans may one day find themselves beginning to live in the cryosphere, climate apocalyptists will undoubtedly dismiss it as a passing aberration.

As for Michael Mann's famous hockey stick graph indicating a spike in recent temperatures, it is a flawed statistical artifact and has been definitively disproved, as A.W. Montford has shown in *The Hockey Stick Illusion: Climategate and the Corruption of Science* (2010). The wrong time scale was used to establish the mean temperature to compare with recorded temperatures of the last century, which accounted for the sudden vertical blade rising from the shaft of a horizontal hockey stick. Professor Mann, it seems, did not account for the Medieval Warming Period between approximately 800 and 1300 C.E. when temperatures were higher than they are today. A hockey stick remains something to play hockey with, not something you fudge a statistical lattice with. Michael Mann has since faced significant legal setbacks, including a judge imposing sanctions against his legal team for alleged misconduct and ordering him to pay over $530,000 in legal fees to his opponents.

Climate warming is an argument that needs to be retired pronto. Pointing to two recent major studies by Scientific Research Publishing and the Journal of Sustainable Development, Catherine Salgado at *PJ Media* writes, correctly: "Climate alarmists have not been right a single time in a major prediction for well over half a century, yet politicians continue to wreak havoc on energy, the economy, education, and other sectors of society and government based on claims of a climate apocalypse that is not coming."

The one thing that is truly warming is the emotional temperature, as well as the rhetoric of the interested parties. If against the evidence we continue to believe that carbon is an evil agent, and if the current anti-carbon delirium should prevail, we are in for a chilling surprise, regardless of our righteous convictions. This is a time for soberly planning how to manage such dismaying contingencies of temperature reduction rather than for accelerating them by helping to cool the planet.

Ignorance may be bliss, but only for a very short while.

16
THE FEVER OF FEMINISM

I f the spirit of the classical Greek playwright Euripides could be summoned from the grave and observe our feminist age, he would not be surprised. In *The Bacchae* (premiered circa 405 B.C.), he told the story of Pentheus, the unfortunate ruler of Thebes, who resisted the ritual incursion of Dionysus, the androgynous god of wine, ecstasy, passionate delirium, and the oracular Mysteries.

In the play, Dionysus returns to Thebes, the city of his birth, accompanied by a retinue of bacchants, or drunken revellers. Finding himself mocked, he infects the women of the royal household with an access of divine frenzy, whereupon they flee into the forest to perform paroxysms of fevered worship. Pentheus wishes to preserve the functioning of the state and recognizes that the upsurge of visionary dementia and phobic irrationality exemplified by the maenads or "raving ones" —the RadFem hordes of the day—would lead to the disruption of the political order and the destabilization of civil society.

Pentheus intends to put an end to the insanity but, influenced by Dionysus, falls prey to curiosity and is persuaded to disguise himself in women's clothing, enter the forest and witness the maenadic revels from a perch in a tall fir tree. He is spotted by the tribe of hysterics, brought to the ground and ripped to shreds, the mordancy of the scene enhanced by the fact that it is his own mother, Agave, who tears off his head and carries the trophy back to Thebes.

Of course, the play is far more complex than this short synopsis would indicate. Euripides treats the perennial conflict between the Olympian gods and the maternal Furies, between man and woman, between social order and individual enthusiasm, between Apollo, the god of reason and light, and Dionysus representing the darker forces of emotion and rapture—or as we would say today, of libido. In Freudian terms, it is the struggle between the Superego and the Id.

This theme was famously addressed by Euripides' great predecessor Aeschylus in the *Oresteian Trilogy*, where the female goddesses the *Eumenides* (or Furies) are pitted against the male Olympians. Both forces, Aeschylus felt, the visceral and the rational, were necessary to the proper conduct of the state and the life of the individual, but must be contained in a condition of approximate balance to avoid a descent into anarchy. The message of The Bacchae, however, is ambiguous insofar as the conclusion of the play suggests the desired victory of the Dionysian infatuation, yet the disintegration of public order and Apollonian statecraft would have been obvious to Euripides' audience. We recall that Plato's *Republic*, in which music, art, and trance-like phenomena were to be the prohibited by law, appeared circa 380 B.C., only 25 years after the initial performance of The Bacchae. Both sides of the dynamic had their dedicated votaries.

Perhaps it was ever thus as one or another of these indispensable forces inevitably comes to predominate. Indeed, the Greek tragedians seemed to understand that the battle between male structure and female sentiment was an eternal fact of human life. For Aeschylus, to privilege one over the other ends in disaster— "Either way, ruin," as Orestes laments in the first play of the Trilogy, a phrase adopted by the philosopher G.W.F. Hegel in his *Lectures on*

Aesthetics as a capsule definition of tragedy. For Euripides, the labile spirit of the feminine must be released into the world, whatever the cost. Yet, despite the priority given to Dionysus and his "agenda," there are, as it were, strong premonitory elements in *The Bacchae* that apply to our contemporary dilemma in which carceral feminism has come to cultural prominence.

In the current historical moment, the trance afflicting our radical feminists is not imposed from without, as in the play, but is self-induced, leading to a nationwide vendetta against so-called "toxic masculinity."

The belief that the "patriarchy" is responsible for all of society's ills has produced destructive consequences: the ubiquitous allegations targeting men for sexual misconduct on the flimsiest of pretexts, the reduction of normative sexuality to the status of an aberration or a crime, the shunting of jurisprudence away from the English Common Law principle of "burden of proof" toward the dodgy concept of "preponderance of evidence" (i.e., whatever the adjudicator feels is likely or credible, almost always in favor of the female plaintiff), the campaign to Ritalin young male students into a state of narcolepsy, the precipitous decline of male university graduates, and the accelerating collapse of the institution of marriage. Contemporary feminists are Euripidean maenads in modern form, metaphorically and, in social effect, tearing men limb from limb in a fury of pathogenic derangement.

What is also interesting is that Pentheus allows himself to be persuaded to wear female attire, ma ruler in drag, in order to carry out his reconnaissance unobserved. Mutatis mutandis, a version of his regrettable decision is currently flourishing among us when men come increasingly to side with the feminist prepossession—judges, teachers, political leaders, university administrators, intellectuals, talking heads, all supporting the feminist dogma that women are society's innocent victims and men violent oppressors and ruthless demagogues who must be denounced, punished, brought low like

Pentheus from his tree, and ultimately feminized.

Men now find themselves in a binary Penthean condition: on the one hand, the profusion of beta males sporting their inner maenadic vestments—*aka* manginas and "white knights," emanations of the god whose epithets include *Dionysos Dimorphos* (dual-formed), *gunnis* (womanish man), and *pseudanor* (counterfeit man); and on the other, men who wish to remain men being culturally dismembered and socially castrated. The balance between the sexes, both biological and cultural, is now communally distorted beyond recognition as Dionysus celebrates his triumph over Apollo and the Furies swarm Mount Olympus.

"It is precisely Dionysus' identification with the feminine," writes classical scholar Froma Zeitlin in *Sexuality and Gender in the Classical World*, that allows the god to introduce "confusions, conflicts, tensions and ambiguities" into the hierarchical masculine world, thus disrupting "the normal social categories" and impairing male confidence and authority to the detriment of the whole. This is where we have arrived in our era of Dionysian madness.

The issue at stake is a perennial one, even more pertinent today then it was in classical Greece. In a late play (392 B.C.) *Assembly of Women (Ecclesiazusae)*, the Greek comic playwright Aristophanes and contemporary of Euripides humorously pilloried the female takeover of the Athenian Assembly and dominion over the wider cultural domain. Its instigator, the early feminist firebrand Praxagora, manages to persuade her beta-male husband Blepyrus of the virtues of female control and convinces the male Assembly to hand over the reins of power to their women. The results are as hilarious in context as they are predictable in the larger world, a society descending into mayhem, pagan ritual, lack of distinction and ruthless feuding for freebies, including sexual favors for unattractive hags at the expense of their more beautiful rivals—an apposite metaphor for the war between merit and mediocrity, reason and sentiment, the Olympian and the Chthonic, as the Greek dramatists understood it.

Scholar and translator Robert Mayhew summarizes in his rendition of the play, "Misery is not abolished, it is merely redistributed." Dionysus prevails.

As Agave laments at the end of *The Bacchae*, "It was Dionysus who proved our ruin; now I see it all." In demanding obeisance to temperamental fury at the expense of the principle of order, feminists and their allies have unleashed a storm of discontent, resentment, misrule, and social turmoil whose consequences will be catastrophic. Without the reassertion of proud and inherent masculinity to restore the equilibrium between the sexes, the road to political suicide and cultural decay is wide open and we will all, women as well as men, suffer for it.

17
THE PARSIFAL TRAP

With every minor political victory, my conservative friends never fail to inform me that the tide is turning. I've been fed this dinning phrase so often, and have seen it written so many times, that I sometimes imagine the tide finally twisting itself into a nautical pretzel. Much conservative hope seems to be awash in slack water which never quite manages to reverse direction.

For the last ten years a good friend has seen the tide turn with every occasion of potentially good news—a perpetrator convicted for a crime rather than his victim for self-defence, a wife arrested for assaulting her husband rather than the husband for being assaulted, a refugee jailed for rape rather than the woman cited for provocation, and so on. That such events are practically a null hypothesis never occurs to her.

Another friend is, I'm sad to say, an inveterate conspiracy nut. A secret society of Rosicrucians is steering the political world toward freedom and prosperity, as witness the events in Italy, El Salvador and Argentina. The rest of the world cannot be far behind. Moreover, Donald Trump is in control of the American melodrama, arranging for his own legal troubles to impress the electorate with his targeted innocence before emerging from every litigation in ascendant glory, a sure sign of the victory of good over evil. The positive evidence is everywhere to be seen, apparently. One need only know where to look to assure oneself that Trump will inevitably overcome the margin of fraud, even though the corrupt judiciary declares it will continue to prosecute him.

Another old friend, a poet of noble inclinations, believes that since the Liberal Party of Canada is generous to its artists, it will eventually reconsider its autocratic ways, move along a more socially conservative track and, therefore, merit our vote. Indeed, the election of a decent Liberal backbencher of his acquaintance is a clear signal that the tide is turning. That Canada's artistic and poetic communities consistently vote Liberal while earnestly denouncing the Conservatives, and that the decent Liberal backbencher votes along party lines and has never introduced a private member's bill, reveal that a presumed sign of civic benefits is a symptom of its opposite, and that my friend is a casualty of his own folly.

Two of my correspondents each sent me an internet facsimile of a page from Klaus Schwab's COVID 19: *The Great Reset* in which Schwab inveighs against a society of "useless eaters." Now Schwab is a problematic individual in league with a cenacle of globalists and oligarchs bent on demolishing the democratic order of nations, but he never used the phrase "useless eaters." That particular page cannot be found in his text. Neither of my correspondents had read Schwab's book but were only too eager to believe the wind was in their sails and to credit a forgery as authentic, harming both their credibility and the validity of the conservative argument.

These are only a few examples from a lengthy catalogue of tide-turners. They express a psychological tropism I believe is common to much conservative thinking, always quick to snatch promise from unlikelihood, or at any rate, fantasy from reality, proof that conservative analysis is often unreliable and is prone to underestimating the cleverness and determination of the Left.

This is not to say that reason and right are contraindicated, only that many conservatives seem inherently liable to moon-muddle. Good things do happen. But it should be acknowledged that conservative policies supporting freedom, faith and family can prevail only at intervals and only if one recognizes the unbending nature of the reality principle against which one must continue to struggle.

One recalls that old saw about the arc of the moral universe bending toward justice. The phrase goes back to Martin Luther King's celebrated conviction that "the arc of the moral universe is long, but it bends toward justice," a mythologem which derives in turn from a sermon delivered in 1853 by the American transcendentalist preacher Theodore Parker, who confessed, "I do not pretend to understand the moral universe. The arc is a long one . . . And from what I see I am sure it bends toward justice."

I, for one, am not so sure. Evil, I am convinced, is the default condition of the human world, which John of Patmos in the *Book of Revelation* portrayed as a demonic force and Thomas Aquinas in the *Summa* defined as a lack or emptiness in the core of the self. It entails the exercise of malignity, whether motiveless or not. It is something we can surmount only intermittently and only if we understand that we live in a state of neap tide and that the arc of the moral universe is more of a wavering line. The tide never quite turns and the arc never quite bends—in any event, not this side of heaven.

Regrettably, for a certain stamp of the conservative mind, the tide is always turning and the arc is always bending—although there is no indication of the process ever being completed. This is what I call the Parsifal trap. Parsifal—the "innocent fool" of the Grail legend—initially believes that justice and reason are present to be readily grasped and that the world is a fundamentally decent place. In the words of mythographer and psychologist Robert A. Johnson, "It would take years of grueling, rigorous battles and quests" before Parsifal arrives at the mature realization that the real world is difficult, complex and resistant, requiring a degree of skepticism and modesty, as well as courage, if one is to come to terms with it and achieve a modicum of success. "Parsifal need only ask the right question." In other words, one interrogates experience with scrupulous candor to find what is there rather than seek for confirmation of one's biases or snag a desired conclusion from an obscure and enigmatic world.

Once this fact is understood and absorbed, conservatives are less likely, to quote Robert Ludlum's *The Parsifal Mosaic*, a serious thriller about the isolated and always insecure triumph of grit in a theater of perpetual violence and malfeasance, "to build delusions out of images and fantasies out of abstractions." Those conservatives who tend to interpret every dixie cup as the Holy Grail must come to understand things may improve, if only temporarily, assuming political and practical affairs are approached with some degree of self-deprecation and sincerity of purpose.

Perseverance, prudence and, let's say, clinical rather than romantic analysis, are the antidotes to the eclipse of hope and the erosion of constructive effort. This is a lesson many conservatives need to learn. The adversary may be absurd or insane, but the adversary is formidable and relentless. Parsifal needs to grow up and transcend the handicap of uninstructed innocence.

18
A Night in Casablanca

Once upon a time, when I was visiting Casablanca and strolling about the streets at all hours, I came upon a company of six or seven students in a public souk cramming for their end-of-term examinations. It was two o'clock in the morning. These kids were so poor they had to avail themselves of the electric lighting in the city squares to do their late-night studying. They were the joint owners of one used and battered book, a copy of André Gide's *L'Immoraliste*, which they passed between them from hand to hand like the Gray Sisters' single eye in the Greek myth; it was their window on the world of literary scholarship.

As I happened to be familiar with the text, having taught it several times in the past, I was invited to deliver an impromptu lecture-and-seminar on Gide and his complex relationship to North Africa. Feeling a little like Robert McCrum, as he recounts in *Globish*, lecturing extemporaneously before an informal klatch of Chinese students, I took what seemed at first like a rather precarious plunge. But as McCrum writes, "the mood [was] unquenchably relaxed, friendly and inspired by a common purpose."

An unprepared teaching session transacted in a second language—French—with an improvisational class in the middle of the night in a strange and remote country proved to be a decisive pedagogical moment, almost a conversion experience, which I have never forgotten. The colloquy lasted until sunrise after which we adjourned to a small café to continue the discussion over coffee. Finally, I was escorted back to my hotel where we exchanged well wishes and good-byes, both teacher and students conscious of the fact that something extraordinary—and yet entirely natural—had just occurred.

I have rarely encountered a group of more committed students, struggling under crushing disadvantages, yet diligent in their outlook, applying themselves to mastering the same text that my own students tended to write off as just another irrelevant book, better managed under the auspices of Monarch Notes. These young people, for whom a park bench did duty as a library carrel, were, obviously, studying to pass a test. But what affected me most was the sense of conviction and desire, the disinterested (not uninterested) passion they brought to bear upon the text.

They were in love with learning, grateful for the privilege of staying up all night to listen to a teacher, trade ideas, ask questions, range far beyond the designated field of practical inquiry governed by the impending test, track connections with other books and writers (including St. Augustine, who was North African). In order to pursue their education, they considered it normal to work double time and more: none had fewer than two jobs, and two had become male prostitutes to finance their studies. Several were providing for their sisters. And they could believe only with difficulty my account of the indifference and torpor that vitiated perhaps a majority of my middle-class students' academic "careers." The contrast was, to put it mildly, instructive.

My own students enjoyed heat in the winter and plentiful electric lighting at all times, owned their own books (often sold back to the bookstore at term end, as they saw no point in keeping them), had unlimited access to libraries, and benefitted where necessary from plentiful loans and scholarships to assist them in pursuing their studies. Yet their enthusiasm for learning could not even remotely compare with what I was observing in an unfurnished, late-night public square. What I intuited then and fully apprehend now is that without a more or less equivalent degree of responsibility and determination on our part, an awareness of the value of literary studies and an ethical commitment to mastering our intellectual history and incorporating the wisdom and intelligence of the larger culture that ultimately sustains (or sustained) us, the world in which we live and which we take for granted will surely founder.

This caveat applies equally to that portion of the teaching profession that has eagerly surrendered to the romantic notion of student "empowerment" —another way of victualing the depressing status quo by refusing to teach genuine ways of learning—and that is busy promoting the subversion of authority, precedence, personal independence, intellectual rigor, and the quest for determinate truth. These teachers' pedagogical rationale operates under the general rubrics of "social justice" and "postmodern indeterminacy." They tend to be regarded as "experts in the field," but as Primo Levi said in *The Monkey's Wrench*, "I never saw an expert who was any good." Regrettably, we cannot rely on a scattering of Moroccan students to march to our salvation.

The tacit bond between teacher and student has now started to unravel. The covenant between the participants in the noble pursuit of intellectual discourse must be predicated on the assumption of a possible mutual ideality, a striving to disengage the best self from the turmoil of appetitive claims and desires that obscure it. The teacher has to assume the role of committed intercessor, and the student needs to be willing to suspend an increasingly fashionable skepticism about the importance of humanistic scholarship and to struggle against the blandishments of a high-tech, instantaneous, digital milieu that will infallibly bankrupt him or her both materially and spiritually.

At the same time, many teachers have, by now, given up or become disablingly skeptical. Others teach not the curriculum but a politically correct travesty of what passes for genuine knowledge — "Taqiyya for Kids," as Janet Tassel calls it in *American Thinker*, or Howard Zinn's treasonably distorted history of the United States. A disturbing number of students have lapsed into a coma from which all too few seem likely to awaken. With a handful of redeeming exceptions, writers pander or traffic in technicalities. Like the students they once were, most readers wish to be stroked, not struck.

The decline of education, which means also the fading out of historical memory and the dimming of literate curiosity, has been the case for some considerable time now. The insistent question is: how does one go about trying to rescue a culture in the throes of custodial dissolution? Over the years I have regularly set my students (rather lenient) tests in general knowledge and particularly in Canadian history; with one exception, I found myself unable in good conscience to award a single passing grade.

And what is one to make, for example, of the fact that someone like Canada's quondam minister of Defense, John McCallum, who holds degrees from several prestigious universities, had never heard of the disastrous raid on the beaches of Dieppe until the moment came to mark its 60th anniversary? In a letter sent by the Minister to the *National Post* claiming to have been misinterpreted, Mr. McCallum referred to the WW I victory at Vimy Ridge as having occurred at Vichy, capital of the Nazi puppet regime in occupied France during WW II. This is the same McCallum who also alluded to the threat of war between India and Afghanistan.

Then we have the fiasco of former Liberal Prime Minister Paul Martin, who delivered a speech to the military base in Gagetown, New Brunswick, on April 14, 2004, in which he twice praised the Canadian effort in the 1944 invasion of *Norway*. A monument erected in Port Hope, Ontario as part of the Highway of Heroes project, honoring 67 individuals who "paid the ultimate sacrifice," included errors that misrepresented military service records, the names of those who were still alive, had died of natural causes, or never saw combat. Typical.

One is also reminded of President Obama's notorious gaffes —the Austrian language, the 57 (or 58) states, "corpsman" pronounced as "corpseman," the identification of the Malvinas as the Maldives, Hawaii as part of Asia, the Muslim history of Cordoba set in the period of the Inquisition, etc. Senator Hank Johnson believed that the island of Guam was in danger of capsizing due to the weight of military equipment and personnel. Mayor of Philadelphia Cherelle Parker spells the name of the city's football team, the Eagles, as "ELGSES." One recalls the flap under the 1999 administration of Washington, D.C. mayor Anthony Williams over the perfectly good word "niggardly," which cost an official his job after a black colleague was offended by its use.

Clearly, the failure of both memory, knowledge and general smarts has become ubiquitous, illustrations of *bioleninism* at work— the building of positions of authority from an underclass of the inept. (Though, extrapolating from renowned historian Robert Conquest's 2006 interview with *Radio Free Europe*, it should really be called biostalinism. "Stalin certainly produced a system under which duller and duller and stupider and stupider people came to the top," he says, "But that isn't based on Lenin's system.")

One recalls, too, in this connection the British company Umbro, which outfits the English national soccer team, that marketed the Zyklon running shoe, unaware until controversy erupted of the Zyklon B poison gas the Nazis used in the concentration camps. "We are sure that the name was not meant to cause offense," explained an Umbro spokesman, whose own name is Nick Crook.

No less disturbing is a student paper I read in which the writer claimed that "man descended from the trees around two hundred years ago and experienced the Enlightenment." I was initially baffled by the phrase "the turtle hypodermic of sickenpods" in another paper, until I learned that the student meant "the total epidemic of psychopaths." (I later adopted the phrase as a book title.) These are only a few examples, among the many thousands bristling in my personal files culled from every walk and profession of life, of the intellectual eclipse that has overtaken us. The level of ignorance is stupefying and, I have come to believe, barring a miracle, verging on the irreparable.

In an excellent article for *PJ Media*, Victor Davis Hanson laments the decay of serious reading in the contemporary West. "The mind is a muscle," he writes, and "without exercise it reverts to mush." The mental brownout he is analyzing afflicts not only our technoliterate youth, but even members of Congress whose speeches "almost require[ ] a translator." Literature, he reminds us, "endows us not just with a model of expression and thought, but also with a body of ideas" —which is grievously lacking among our contemporaries. The technical devices on which we pride ourselves "speed up communication, but can slow down thought." He concludes, and I quote in full: "Somehow we must convince this new wired generation that speaking and writing well are not just the DSL lines of modern civilization, but also the keys to self-mastery, a sort of code that one takes on—in addition to others, moral and legal—to uphold standards of culture itself, to keep the work and ideas alive of our long gone betters for one more generation—as if to say, 'I did my part according to my time and station.' Nothing more, nothing less."

Nothing more, nothing less. Each of us committed to the regeneration of a mushy and degraded culture must find some way, hope against hope, to engage those who have surrendered to the zeitgeist. There are several ways of doing this: in diligent conversation with students and friends, in writing cogent and fact-based articles and books, or in adhering to the principles of real, honest-to-goodness teaching. Working to put paid to the government's education monopoly, that is, embarking on a movement favoring market-driven education over its state-run counterpart, can be, in the words of Henry Lever of the Mises Institute. "a victory from which all other victories follow."

In my own practice as a teacher, I decided it might be fruitful to hold optional weekend seminars in my home, in which my students and I would discuss, among other things, the deterioration of reading in the current cultural climate and what we could do about it. Some of these students agreed to allow me to check on their progress after they graduated, to keep longitudinal tabs on them. All expressed their gratitude for those "Sabbath" classes in our living-room souk.

One of my subjects, now the manager of a rock band, called after a silence of some years from a bar in the backwater town of Trois Rivières in Quebec to discuss Hermann Hesse's psychedelic novel, *Journey to the East*. The fact that my former student was under the influence of something other than Miller Lite seemed appropriate in the narrative circumstance. He may have been floating in a narcotic reverie; nonetheless, he was struggling with a book.

Maybe that's the best we can hope for now. But at least it's a start.

19
HONORING THE HIGGS

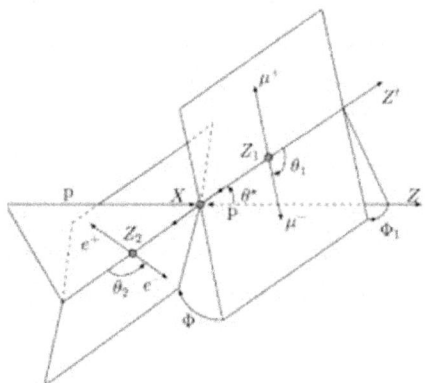

Angular observables sensitive to the spin and parity in
H→ ZZ*→ 4ℓ decay.

Having been interested in science since my university days, I have been following closely the search
for the mysterious, force-carrying Higgs boson, the
so-called "God Particle" that gives nonzero mass to the material
universe in and around us. If the Higgs did not exist, we would be
diaphanous wraiths floating somewhere in the vacuum of space,
virtual creatures popping in and out of existence like quarks and
leptons, quantum nonentities. Of course, we rarely think about the
Higgs, being preoccupied with the business of everyday life and
the projects we are invested in. Yes, politics is important, financial

considerations are essential, art and music and poetry are necessary (or should be), and my embodied wife is the center of my existence. But that is all thanks to the Higgs boson.

Physics theory predicts the existence of the Higgs boson (which includes the Higgs Field and the Higgs Mechanism, but that's for another time). The problem, however, was how to track it down experimentally. Theory is all very well but it needs tangible confirmation, which is what the Large Hadron Collider (LHC) at CERN (European Organization for Nuclear Research) strove to provide. A further problem has to do with the stubborn fact that the Higgs boson can never be seen. It decays too fast and, like the quark, it is a bound particle. It hides in the shadows of sub-atomic transactions that can never be dispelled. It can be known only by the residue, the debris it produces when it "explodes" and scatters, creating a by-product that can be identified as emanating only from the Higgs and no other constituents, and thus affirming its reality. One thinks of Polonius' advice to his servant Reynaldo in *Hamlet*, Act II, Scene 1: "And thus we do of wisdom and of reach/With windlasses and assays of bias/ By indirections find directions out."

There are various ways of producing evidence of the Higgs from targeted particle collisions in high-speed accelerators like the LHC. One method is to smash quarks together to generate a virtual particle that then emits a Higgs boson. Another follows from the emission of two virtual gauge bosons that burst in showers or jets of associated particles. A third event involves the collision of gluons that make two quarks which annihilate and yield a Higgs boson. In each case, the Higgs decays too rapidly to be captured—a lifetime of a tenth of a billion-trillionth of a second—but the distinctive manner of its decay and its remnant products allow it to be detected, by proxy, as it were. This is a vastly oversimplified description of the process—volumes like Leon Lederman's *The God Particle*, Brian Cox and Jeff Forshaw's *the quantum universe*, Lisa Randall's *Higgs Discovery: The Power of Empty Space* and Jim Baggott's *Higgs: The Invention and*

Discovery of the 'God Particle', among dozens of others, furnish excellent source material. (Spoiler Alert: the subject is addictive.)

But the Higgs and the methods adopted for its discovery interest me for other reasons as well. Poet Gerard Manley Hopkins wrote: *O the mind, mind has mountains; cliffs of fall / Frightful, sheer, no-man-fathomed.* True enough, but the mind is also like a large hadron collider, confirming theory by examining its scattered and far-flung empirical manifestations. When the mind is functioning as it should, it follows a similar hunt-and-find procedure as employed at CERN, formulating theory from certain givens and searching for its disparate products in the external, material world to test its validity.

Pertinent results naturally presume that the cerebral LHC is working properly and that it is able to detect the real-world detritus that also confirms what we may call the "Devil's Particle," extrapolating from Paul Kengor's *The Devil and Karl Marx*. Kengor followed the same modus operandi, studying the disjected litter of a broken symmetry created by smashing together the texts and theories of a given ideological movement, the secular left and the devastation it causes, breaking eggs to make an omelet that never comes together and remains inedible. In so doing, he exposes the force-bearing utopian particle that gives weight and heft to a disruptive ideology. Of course, the species of Higgs I'm describing here is a multifactorial particle, a mental boson that cannot be seen or grasped but gives substance to social, political and economic phenomena in the world we create around us, for better or for worse. It can be investigated by distinguishing the branching rules governing its couplings with real-world phenomena.

As it should go without saying, I am only proposing a model of deductive/inductive thinking—sequent logic and retrolinear congruence—as it pertains to all fields, subjects and intellectual endeavors. It's an obvious metaphor of how the mind functions when it doesn't "quench" —a term used at CERN when the apparatus erratically shuts down. As Samuel Taylor Coleridge wrote in his *Bi-*

ographia Literaria, "No metaphor runs on all four legs." Clearly, neither does this one.

But my fascination with the Higgs in its diverse applications remains. The miracle of an infinitesimal scalar generating a world of macro vectorials is surely something to celebrate. I regard the Higgs as a friend, my boson buddy, as we should all. It allows one to play with the concept, to indulge in fanciful speculations, to have what I think of as "explanatory fun," and to do real, not pretend, science. More seriously, it is also a benefactor, for without the interactions of the Higgs I wouldn't be here to fly this squib and you wouldn't be here to shoot it down. It enables us to pursue the ideas, preoccupations, fetishes, commitments and projects that give our lives meaning and purpose and amusement, as well as to demolish theories and assumptions that have no purchase on observable adequacy. It takes precedence. A spin 0 particle has conferred nonzero presence upon us. Will wonders never cease! It puts things in perspective.

So we must be grateful, in the words of Murray Gell-Mann from *The Quark and the Jaguar,* for "the mechanism that breaks the symmetry of the zero-mass approximation and is responsible for the various different non-zero particle masses in the standard model." It is the initial condition that allows for the reality and expansion of our lives. The Higgs deserves our attention and respect. It is the author of Non Zero.

20

THE CHANGE IN
DONALD TRUMP

J ust this morning, watching a political news video, I noticed a well set-up gentleman walking into camera range.
The camera focused briefly on his face and I thought to
myself that the man bore a close resemblance to Donald Trump.
Suddenly I realized it was Donald Trump, but something about him
had demonstrably changed. His gait was slower, more deliberate,
and the expression on his face was more solemn, less mobile, altogether less lively and mutable. He did not look quite like himself,
but far more serious, more like a chess grandmaster or a sage in
contemplation. I'm sure other Trump-spotters had experienced the
same sense of disorientation and at least mild bewilderment.

And why not? One recalls the famous quote from Samuel
Johnson: "Depend on it, sir, when a man knows he is to be hanged
in a fortnight, it concentrates his mind wonderfully." *Mutatis mutandis*, a bullet intended for a man's head and providentially slicing off
part of an ear, even if he escaped death, will have a profound effect
on a man's perspective on the world and his emotional valence, as
well as on his physical demeanor.

The bombast and sarcasm and occasional vulgarities which
many found irritating and others entertaining and down to earth,
the flamboyant and boisterous self-presentation, the raucous good

humor as well as the incendiary comments, the pointing finger singling out friends in the audience, the up-tempo disco moves that swept the world, the tics and mannerisms of a man accustomed to performing—all these have been supplemented by an attitude of sobriety and somber thoughtfulness. Trump had become, as they like to say, increasingly "presidential." "The Donald J. Trump who took the stage in Milwaukee," writes Stephen Kruiser at *PJ Media*, "was a reflective, determined elder statesman . . . Trump's *sotto voce*, conversational tone was perfect, and a counter to the angry maniac that the commies in the mainstream media like to portray him as." *The Spectator World*, an unfriendly outfit, also alluded to a "new subdued Trump."

In *The Varieties of Religious Experience*, William James elaborates on a distinction made by classical scholar Francis Newman between the once-born and the twice-born. "God has two families of children on this earth," said Newman, "the once-born and the twice-born." The once-born are simple, vigorous, physically assertive, and have faith in a perfectible universe. The twice-born have been somehow transformed, aware of the deeper mysteries of life, the refractory nature of mankind, and the incongruities and absurdities that rule over the political and social theaters. "He or she has become painfully aware of the dark realities of existence.?"

James considers a personal crisis that transformed the life of Leo Tolstoy, author of *War and Peace*, as follows: "The process is one of redemption, not of mere reversion to natural health, and the sufferer, when saved, is saved by what seems to him a second birth, a deeper kind of conscious being than he could enjoy before." It is something "haunting, abiding and oppressive," wrote the Victorian savant and economist Walter Bagehot in *Literary Studies*, "that changes men's inner lives and makes them receptive to the idea of God." It is obvious that Trump now belongs to the family of the twice-born. As he confided, "That was an amazing, horrible thing. Amazing thing. And in many ways, it changes your attitude, your viewpoint on life. And I think, honestly, I think you appreciate God even more. I really do."

The question for many of us is which Trump do we prefer: the once-born gladiator who battled in the octagon of bloody UFC-type politics, dynamic, utterly confident, feisty, unorthodox, often exasperating; or the twice-born hero, the quieter, meditative, austere, introspective and dignified champion who no longer fires from the hip but seems rather to be brooding strategically for ultimate victory. Or has he somehow managed to seamlessly combine these two antithetical character traits, a feature of his political genius?

Longtime friend Dana White, president of Ultimate Fighting Championship (UFC), describes Trump as "a fighter . . . the legitimate, ultimate, American badass of all time." I confess I sometimes miss the unfiltered Donald Trump, once affectionately dubbed "the Donald" as if it were the familiar handle of a neighborhood favorite, a bit like Jeff Bridges' "the Dude." But one must also recognize that the stately and pensive survivor of a millimeter attempt on his life is the contemplative and decisive warrior that America—enmeshed in the thickets of identity politics, sexual deviance, feminism, black power and institutional corruption springing from the ideological roots of the Left—now desperately needs.

21
INFANTALIZING
THE ACADEMY

Not long ago, I was asked by an Italian author and journalist, working on an article for *Il Giorno* on the subject of "mute liberalism" and political correctness in the U.S., for my impressions of the "decadence" afflicting American culture. He wanted to know what the reasons were for what he saw as a political and cultural wasting disease and, in particular, when the inexorable slide began into self-censorship, omnipresent hedonism, the debasement of the social and intellectual elites, the abandonment of republican principles and the reversal of traditional social roles.

This was a question too vanishingly large to answer definitively, but it did get me thinking once again about some of the factors that might have caused—as Québécois producer Denys Arcand put it in the title and story of his sadly amusing film—The *Decline of the American Empire*, a film modelled on Edward Gibbon's *The Decline and Fall of the Roman Empire*.

Decadence, of course, is not solely an American phenomenon; no Western country is exempt from the vectors of degeneration at work in the liberal/democratic sphere today. But what happens to the U.S., as the guarantor of Western freedom and prosperity, happens to the rest of us. With America in decline, none of its dependents—and we are all its dependants, however loath we may be to admit it—will be spared. Indeed, most Western countries can survive their moral and political deterioration so long as America is willing and able to support them militarily, fiscally and politically, which is, for example, the story of ungrateful Europe since the Marshall Plan. Such is no longer the case. This is why the preoccupation of non-nationals—Italians like my interviewer, Canadians like me— with the fortunes of the U.S. is an issue of primary concern.

In any event, the "decadence" my interviewer was referring to obviously began a long time ago—when exactly is another question. One thinks of deconstructionist philosopher Jacques Derrida's theory of receding origins, the elusiveness or "eclipsing structure" of all beginnings. On the American historical scene, one could go back to the slave plantations and the Civil War, to the Salem witch trials, or to the bitter duels inherent in the very Founding of the Republic between central-government Federalists and States-rights Republicans, a dispute that remains a political fracture to this day. Differing understandings of the Greek and Roman classics regarding the nature of enlightened rule and the proper relation between the governing and the governed were also a locus of contention. As Ron Chernow writes in *Alexander Hamilton*, commenting on the discrepancy between intention and result that has never been fully resolved, "Today we cherish the two-party system as a cornerstone of American democracy. The founders, however, viewed parties as monarchical vestiges that had no legitimate place in a true republic." But why stop there? If one wishes, one can go back to the Mayflower and the Arbella and before. A prior "originary" point of decay can always be found.

To focus on the contemporary, certainly John Dewey's left-oriented "progressivist" and "child-centered" education program, developed mainly in *Democracy and Education*, which took root in the 1920s, is a reasonable place to start our investigations. Briefly, Dewey believed the child should never be "forced" to learn but rather encouraged to follow his own natal interests—a theory earlier elaborated in the Romantic school of poetry, for example, William Wordsworth's *Intimations Ode* where we read that the youth "trailing clouds of glory" is "nature's priest," possessing an innate apprehension of the divine. Wordsworth's exaltation of the child melded seamlessly with his revolutionary belief as a young man in the re-pristinizing of society. It comes as no surprise that the Movement's enfant terrible, Percy Bysshe Shelley, who espoused similar sentiments, particularly in poems like *Queen Mab* and *Prometheus Unbound,* earned the praise of Karl Marx. Shelley yearned for the day, as he wrote in Mab, when the "hands/which little children stretch in friendly sport" would become the emblem of a renewed social contract. Dewey's oeuvre was clearly influenced by the rejuvenative assumptions of his nineteenth century Romantic precursors.

Unfortunately, a return to origins or the projection of initial states isn't how the world works. It escaped Dewey's proselytizing ardor that prior learning and hard study, guided by erudite masters, are necessary for a young person to discover what it is in the world that genuinely interests him and what his condign aptitudes really are. Writing in *The Epoch Times,* educator Patrick Keeney points out that "Dewey's principles, especially his emphasis on social engagement, 'relevance,' and personal growth over academic excellence, remain potent in American public education . . . His approach is anti-intellectual and dismissive of traditional educational models," which he denigrated as "Mandarin knowledge." Keeney targets Dewey's "emphasis on the primacy of experiential learning, social engagement, and individual development over the cultivation of intellectual discipline," which he sees as "a direct challenge to the intellectual foundations of education." Only by starting from first principles and shifting away from Dewey's progressive model can the United States hope to restore intellectual rigour and critical thinking in its classrooms.

Such is the only route to maturity, competence and achievement. "Nature's priest" has no future unless he is a prince of learning. Failing to understand the need for pedagogical and curricular discipline, for a wide-ranging and classically imposed syllabus, and opting instead for catering benignity in both the formative and later stages of education is a sure-fire recipe for producing the moral narcissist who is his own only truth. The casualties of this retrograde approach, in Peter Wood's succinct articulation from his online essay "The Architecture of Intellectual Freedom," are "men and women capable of wise and responsible stewardship of a free society."

Dewey's ideas percolated slowly through American culture and took off in the incendiary 60s, with the Free Speech Movement at Berkeley, the psychedelic dumbing down of the youth population, the takeover of the universities by student radicals, and the insidious inroads made by the destabilizing emigré Frankfurt School, especially Herbert Marcuse of "repressive tolerance" fame, who, in essence, popularized the Marxist theories of Antonio Gramsci and Georg Lukács. The world had to be purified by the exploited masses and remade in the image of youthful innocence, a revisionary project that inspired the young, the callow and the doctrinaire. These notions captured the American seminary and poisoned the minds of generations of students. After that, the die was cast, and America was on the road to becoming a European failure.

"Are we not witnessing," asks John Agresto in *Academic Questions* (Vol.29, No.2), "something that looks to be the . . . purposeful eradication of what it has historically meant to be educated?" The mission of the university is now the inculcation of intellectual conformity, a duplicitous "inclusiveness" that banishes dissenting voices, promotes "social justice" and discursive closure, and coddles students into a condition of protracted puberty as the academy devolves into "separate programs of grievance and outrage." In this way, students, stunted in their development, become the shock troops of the new world order as they have been taught to see it. And as we know, and as university policies have made glaringly public, children throw tantrums and don't like to be contradicted.

What we see today, then, universities as centers of leftist in-doctrination, the shutting down of intellectual debate—cf. Allan Bloom's *Closing of the American Mind*— , a generation of "snowflake" students who are preoccupied with frivolities like trigger warnings, microaggresssons, transgender bathrooms, and "safe spaces" where they will never be exposed to an unfamiliar or conflicting idea, and the snivelling infantilization of the entire academic cohort—flows directly from Dewey and his followers. These pedagogical dissidents prepared the ground for the subversive agenda of the Frankfurt-ers by engaging in an act of cerebral softening, that is, elevating the student over the teacher, the child over the man (or woman), and feeling over thought—hence the continuing prominence of the "self-esteem" movement that slashed-and-burned its way through the educational landscape.

One also recalls the baneful influence of Brazilian educator Paulo Freire in his immensely popular *The Pedagogy of the Oppressed*, who argued against the "banking model" of education—students as vessels to be filled, like piggy banks with coins—and insisted that teachers have little to actually teach their students. Their job was to help them to understand their need for liberation from the engines of oppression—a more incendiary version of Dewey's contestation. Adapting the theories of postcolonialist Frantz Fanon's *The Wretched of the Earth*, Freire's Manichean paradigm saw traditional teachers as the colonizers, students as the colonized. The student proletariat was to rise up and seize the means of academic production and, ultimately, the machinery of culture and state.

Thus, students were empowered, staff and administration were intimidated, cognitive regression was guaranteed, and the ed-ucational establishment at all levels, from primary to post-gradu-ate, was critically breached. The K-12 level was populated chiefly by teacher-trained incompetents and fellow-traveling principals who served as the hoplites of the cultural left. The university was now home to a liberal professoriate comprising individuals who adopted the approved dogmatic convictions of the progressivist elect, acquired the appropriate exclusionary jargon, and proceeded to turn their classes into nurseries of ideological pap. With very few current exceptions, like Hillsdale College and the University of Chicago, universities have been unable to resist the annihilationist invasion of political correctness, typified by speech codes, rape hysteria, affirmative action mediocrity (evasively labelled "mismatching"), anti-Western sentiment, and the tendency to totalitarian forms of repression. The general decline in mental acuity, scholarly discipline and historical knowledge was a foregone conclusion, and we are reaping the blighted harvest of that Jacobin declension today.

Indeed, the adolescent fervour for "revolution" damn the consequences was duly convected into the domain of adulthood, as the feral children of the left, whose minds were polluted by the sentimental and reductive theories of the Dewey-inspired and revisionist brigades, graduated into the various positions of cultural authority—media, education, entertainment and government. Our grown-up Magikarps—timid university presidents and academic leaders, the general run of invertebrate politicians and corrupted journalists, the great majority of Hollywood and sports know-nothings—are essentially children, and children cannot hope to survive in a world without real adults, or too few adults to manage the vast playpen that has become almost coterminous with society as a whole. The commonplace adage that the inmates have taken over the asylum is fundamentally mistaken. Rather, the children have taken over the crèche.

Such is the damage the educational institution has wrought in a culture spoiled by affluence and forgetfulness—a culture that has shucked the past and de-realized the future. The falling off from academic integrity and rigor explains why almost everything from political culture to cultural politics smacks increasingly of retardation. And it accounts in large measure for the descent we are observing.

For children, who have no knowledge of the history of their civilization and no sense of an empirical future, cannot think rationally, they can only feel and act upon their feelings. They live in a realm defined by the present and the imaginary. They are the low-information voters, partisan pedants, liberal socialists, leftist ideologues, suborned journalists, ignorant politicians and entitlement parasites of the current day, living in a make-believe world that, failing a course correction, is running out of time.

As conservative thinker Richard Weaver wrote in *Visions of Order*, published in 1964, "without memory and the extrapolation which it makes possible, man becomes a kind of waif" mired in mere presentism. "Under the impossible idea of unrestricted freedom," he continues, "the cry is to bury the past and let the senses take care of the present." As the same time, the future takes on the form of a mythical construct, the dream of a golden age that exists only in the cradles of desire. The upshot is truly alarming: a juvenile public cocooned in the utopian silk of destructive illusions. The waifs appear to have won the day.

A culture or a nation run by children must inevitably falter and decline—unless it can recover its mind and purpose, an eventuality that seems less likely with every passing day. Children always leave a mess behind them that needs to be cleaned up by others, assuming there are enough others around to tackle the job. Children have by their very nature no sense of productive order and plainly no conception of the social, political and economic future. That is why we may not have one.

2 2

GETTING ON
THE GRAVY BOAT

I have consulted Seneca, and if I make
accusations of vanity for this, it seems
that it pleases you to make a villain of me
when it would be better to remain silent.

—Petrarch, *Rime Disperse*, Poem 58

In 1999, Sharon H. Nelson, the author of ten little-known
and largely unreviewed chapbooks dating back to 1972,
received a $20,000 Canada Council Arts Grant to write
a book of poems. Two and half years later an eleven page collection appeared, entitled "How the Soup Gets Made." Not counting
a twelfth page of Notes in which we are given a definition of par-
mentier and a detailed recipe for its preparation, this averages out
to approximately $2000 per page, a sum whose literary amortization
may in this case prove highly problematic.

To get some sense of what this modest work entails, let us
embark on a quick tour of its pages. The book begins with its title
poem where we are initially apprised that

Today I made leek and cauliflower soup
because Brenda had dental surgery this morning . . .

—which is surely a direct if unexpected way of whetting the reader's appetite. While the soup is on the boil, we discover that the poet, speculating over the destiny of her restorative bouillon, is also thinking of

> Rahel and Bella and Maureen,
> all of whom can't eat anything made with allium . . .

and of Maxiane who "no longer eats potatoes." Once we have digested these disturbing facts, however, we learn to our immediate relief that Brenda is recovering well, and soon the steamy kitchen of Nelson's culinary imagination begins to fill with ever more Goddesses of the Soup, a numinous sorority which proceeds to cook soup against the chill,

> and welcome the companionship of friends
> whose presences pervade the air
> with the rising scent of braising vegetables . . .

—the last lines oddly reminiscent of P.G. Wodehouse's parodic Canadian poet, Ralston McTodd, who in *Leave it to Psmith* celebrates "the sibilant, scented silence that shimmered where we sat." (To avoid an olfactory misapprehension, one assumes our poet meant along "with the rising scent.")[1] But the world is a perilous and complicated place and at this point a more sombre and reflective tone asserts itself in a concluding seven-part poem called "Sometimes I Think of You." Now we meet the poet, released from the soup-inspired labours of the kitchen range, meditating at what would appear to be the writing table. Exulting in the "pre-dawn quiet," as the great, abused, resilient women of her lineage were wont to do, the cook turned poet is providentially if temporarily free to apply herself to her more solemn devoirs with

> no small fingers grasping,
> no large hands demanding,
> no mouths to be filled
> besides our own.

Nevertheless, in the quietude of the pre-dawn moment, a dark and

doleful requiem rises suddenly *de profundis* to engulf her shaken spirit and we hear the poet lamenting that, in the crass contemporary
world she is forced to inhabit,

> no one has time
> to use a wooden spoon
> to mix batter for cakes.

She further registers in a striking mix of spondees, pyrrhics, tro-
chees, anapests and iambs that

> small, personal acts of caring
> are abnormal in this age of speed

and, in a burst of typographic inventiveness, notes that

> Love needs
>   a long
>   attention span.

Undeterred, the poet resolves to throw herself heroically into "the
big work"

> as all of us do
> who have not borne
> a dozen children.

The work, presumably equal to that of bearing twelve children, is
cooking, meditating, writing and exchanging little domestic services
with a compatible partner who does the sewing because the poet's
hands

> have been cut and abraded
> by too much kitchen work.

Finally, in the last item of the collection, the poet slippers soft-
ly about in the auroral and preprandial silence, enjoying a "small,
stolen privacy" during which, in a reduced echo of Heine's immortal
"Night Thoughts,"

> sometimes,
> I think of you.

Sometimes I think of Canada and its literary sensibility, whose
granting apparatus can reward authors like Nelson for thirty years

of undistinguished work, and, ultimately for producing not a book of poetry but a potagerie. But of course, it is not only Nelson who can prosper by infliction. For a comparable but more renowned instance of our proud inability to discriminate, we might briefly consider the work of Patrick Lane, a Governor General's Award winning poet ($15,000 in today's currency). Lane's most recent book, *The Bare Plum of Winter Rain*, is one of the more embarrassing examples of the verbal tripe Canadian poets are inclined to serve up to their readers. And while soup doesn't figure on Lane's menu, macaroni certainly does, as the poet's wife

> at the grey stove
> spooned the pale bare curls
> unto each plate,

and the poet danced

> Around the table . . .
> laughing and singing . . .
> Macaroni, Macaroni!

But the larder Lane remembers seems a rather depleted one, for the plum (tree?) is also bare. How one longs in contrast for the "fragrant plum tree/of joyousness and talk" of the Japanese master Soin's famous starting-piece and recalls with gratitude and relief Wallace Stevens' assurance in "The Comedian As The Letter C" that "The plum survives its poems." Yet, plums aside, even if the apples Lane once carried in his hands are "rusted and tired from their lives," the poet in a fit of nostalgia would still want to go back in order

> to eat the lunch we ate that day,
> baloney sandwiches—bread, margarine, and baloney
> and cold coffee we'd saved from morning . . .

The savor of the exiguous is very strong in Lane, the poet of night, hunger, loneliness and poverty—in a word, of cold coffee and old baloney—who in poem after poem reveals to the world a deeply troubled spirit that strives to compensate for loss by celebrating the

plenitude of the vanishing moment in the storied intimacy of encounter. The balladeer of deprivation is then subtly but inexorably
transformed into the minnesinger of abundance. This is probably
why as we move through the book we find the table gradually replaced by the bed and the miracles of profusion that can be performed thereon. Thus, in a poem entitled "Cunt," the poet, like the
most adroit of magicians, rummages from his lover's nether cor-
nucopia all sorts of unprecedented objects, such as a crow's wing,
a wolf's paw, a doll without eyes, an unborn walrus tusk, a little
sequoia nut, the finger-bone of a mouse and a pig's hoof—a nonpa-
reil cunt whose fertility is clearly more than equal to the poet's and
reconciles him to life's fragility and destitution. One might almost
expect a copy of "How the Soup Gets Made" to emerge from that
capacious orifice. (The notorious Mary Tofts, who in 1726 began to
extrude parts of animals, the legs of a cat, sundry sooterkins and
nine baby rabbits all in one go, pales in comparison.) The following
poem in the collection breathlessly compares his lover's vulva to
"the flutter of many soft petals," the "whispering of the solitary
dove" and "the open mouth of praise," closing with the incantation
"Vulva, vulva." Love or some facsimile thereof is all you need, apparently.

Even the girls in his Creative Writing class—a class in which
sentiment and innocence demonstrably substitute for hard work
and ruthless self-evaluation—come in for instant poetic consecra-
tion. Being "everything I love," these students

> place their stories on the page
> and though some of their poems are dark
> they always bring a light
> to heal what might have broken them
>
> when they were only girls: lost love,
> lost lives, lost innocence. They are witness
> to what they know and they tell us
> that we might hear and be made whole at last.

The context is the infamous massacre of fourteen young women at the University of Montreal by a crazed misogynist, a context whose absolute horror renders Lane's milking of his audience for sympathy and approval in a facile, unworked poem like "What Breaks Us" practically obscene. But the poet's love continues to flow like the proverbial milk and honey, an elixir that has nothing in common with Frost's cold brook in "Directive" from whose waters we may "Drink and be whole again beyond confusion" —a well-known line which Lane's poem consciously or unconsciously reprises. Finally, in the concluding piece, "The Sealing" (which begins somewhat disingenuously, albeit with Bondean panache: "This is for your eyes alone"), he hands over his poems to his companion while unblushingly cascading her in clichés:

> You are the one I made
> them for, in the quiet of my room,
> in the dead of the night.

After so many fascinating disclosures, I do not want to mince words. For these and other sadly unindictable offenses he was recently awarded a $20,000 Canada Council Arts Grant.

The only salient distinction between Lane and Nelson is that one is highly acclaimed and the other is not, but between these two exemplary poets falls the shadow of our endowed ineptitude. Now if people wish to write poetry, they should certainly not be prevented from doing so. If the poetry turns out to be rebarbatively bad, Stephen King's Langoliers will eventually take care of matters and it will be as if it had never been published. I would ask my reader to understand that I have no quarrel as such with Nelson's poetic ladlings or Lane's lexical upchuckings even if they happen to be representative of much of the rubbish regularly written and published by the majority of the country's poets—the only real difference between the two, as suggested above, being that poets like Nelson happen to be advantageously obscure. Since her poems are unread, the fact that a national granting organization is profoundly implicated in underwriting such irrelevancies goes unsuspected and largely unexposed.

My quarrel, then, is not so much with the poet as with the dispensing agency that allows for such work to be produced and disseminated. The state in which the granting structure now malingers is nothing short of outrageous. If an officially accredited institution charged with nurturing and protecting the country's literature can impenitently disburse exorbitant sums to foster poets like Nelson and Lane—or Penn Kemp, Daphne Marlatt, Diana Hartog, Esta Spalding and Jeff Derkson, to name only a few of the big winners in Canada Council competitions over the last few years—then it is time to reconsider and take stock. Some of these writers are well known and others are not, but they are all equally weak and undeserving. For our poets have come progressively to resemble in their own humble way the CEOs of great corporations who profit from cashed stock options and golden handshakes for leading their firms into bankruptcy. Career plainly takes precedence over achievement and what is generated for our consumption is a flat and insipid poetry that does not struggle to come into the world but is effortlessly grubstaked into existence. Thus it is not only a question of the waste of public funds that I am raising here but of the indelible impression of vacancy which such an incompetent, closed and self-interested adjudication process leaves in its aftermath.

For we have to face the fact that the jury system as it is presently constituted, especially in the notoriously litigious field of Canadian poetry, is essentially nothing more than a private club of pork-barrel literary politicos involved in prosecuting personal vendettas, settling old scores, rewarding friends and acolytes, and establishing a kind of identity agenda, whether regional, feminist or programmatic. With respect to these latter categories, it is no secret that Westcoast writers tend to receive a lot of grants; so do feminists and so-called language poets. An article in *Quill & Quire* (July 2001) provides a table of the cash values of awards disbursed between 1991 and 2000. There we discover, for example, that during the decade in question Patrick Lane was subsidized to the tune of $154,550, Susan Musgrave had to settle for $152,450 and Audrey Thomas (though not a poet) is learning to make do with a mere huckle of $122,000. (Musgrave constitutes a special case for despite her abominable poetry on the one hand and her obviously superb grant-writing skills on the other there is an endearing side to her too; anyone who tries, if the story is true, to deposit money for her husband's defense fund in the same bank he had recently robbed deserves our sympathy.) Brian Brett, poor sod, is struggling to survive at a derisory $88,632. So much for the West-coasters. As for the other niches I touch upon, one notes in passing that Judith Fitzgerald heads the list at $154,750, Lynn Crosbie is chugging along at $90,850, and Marlene NorbeSe Philip continues to bear eloquent witness to an unfair and problematic world at a cost to the taxpayer of $89,184. (She has, as of this writing, received a further $20,000 from the Ontario Arts Council to provide a "historic re-telling" of the voyage of a slave ship.) This is a most chastening spectacle: poets going after perks with the blunt appetite of a mullet snouting up flounder eggs. Not a pretty image, but I have seen both and the resemblance is startling. Everything considered, perhaps we should be grateful for Nelson's comparatively modest endorsement.

The reason, obviously, for the systemic distortions I have been targeting is that the jurors assembled by the Council inevitably become tightly-knit special-interest groups intent on pursuing votary policies accountable to no larger community or supervening authority and abetted by the serene indifference of a glabrous bureaucracy. Their motives range across the entire gamut of debatable objectives, from multicultural tokenism to private allegiance to a sort of displaced quid pro quo psychology, the secret spring of most conciliar outcomes in the area of literary competitions no less than in Olympic skating. The occasional astute judgments these juries render— in part owing to chance and the law of averages—are effectively obliterated by the dopey and partisan decisions they are increasingly prone to make.

The unpleasant truth is that, given the hothouse and incestuous nature of our literary climate, one year's jurors will invariably resurface as another year's applicants, so that what we are really doing is playing musical grants, installing a system of personal arrangements in which a coterie of predatory triflers are allowed to perpetuate both their circulating emoluments and the frowsty, predictable quality of a nation's literature. A letter I recently received from a Canadian periodical editor spells out the problem clearly. He mentions two well-known literary figures who agreed fully with a negative critique of a celebrated poet I had just published but who refrained from coming out of the closet in support of my argument lest their granting chances be compromised. Nor should it come as any great surprise that a judge on a recent prestigious jury will have had an earlier book of his fulsomely reviewed by both the eventual winner of the contest over which he was presiding and one of its shortlisted nominees. This would explain why we have so many relatively solvent poets incapable of writing a single memorable line in a country that should properly react to their proliferation with shame and aversion rather than the unjustified munificence of a latter day Abimelech. By this time it should be reasonably clear that the reputations of these poets are tied securely to the rusty standards of friendly reviewers, like bicycles chained to parking meters, one wheel missing and the handlebars askew.

I do not wish to imply that there are no fine and meritorious poets to be found among us but that far too many of our clever and industrious scops apparently spend more of their time beavering up grant applications, attending meetings, sitting on tribunals, establishing committees, administering foundations, lobbying for speaking engagements and making profitable contacts than trying to write excellent and reader-responsible poetry.[2] What Horace in the "Ars Poetica" championed as the *aurea mediocritas*, implying that the poet should moderate the claims of the world by giving, not making, profit, has now provided us via the debasement of the word and concept with the green light for unstinted "mediocrity." We should be aware that the truly priceless stuff does not come easy and is always unforeseeable. But bits of refectory lore and, in general, the Canadian staple of personal revelation and hyper-earnest solicitude can be readily purchased at $20,000 a shot and efficiently delivered in time for the beneficiaries to meditate their subsequent applications or reciprocate by making themselves available for jury duty— in some cases even supplicating for Council billetings.

Knowing that any system engaged in the practice of triage, assessment and distribution of public monies or private endowments or a mix of both will be inherently flawed, I am reluctant to propose irreversibly drastic measures to redress the predicament—except to suggest that if a disgrace cannot be rectified, then the circumstances from which it arises should be eliminated. It is, of course, tempting to recommend that the Canada Council—or, say, that department that deals with artists on an individual rather than corporate basis—should be instantly abolished. After all, we need orchestras and theatres and dance companies to provide a locus for collective recreation and cultivation but should remain wary of solo practitioners who claim privileged treatment for vague, arcane and often unascertainable skills. As Robert Allen writes in an essay entitled "Post-Mortemism" (*The Insecurity of Art: Essays on Poetics*), "sometimes I wish the Canada Council did not keep the whole enterprise of poetry going; we would all lose, but the good poets would lose less."

But perhaps one may be somewhat less Jacobin-like and hope that a jury system currently rigged as a parochial cabal might be radically diversified to exclude all practitioners of the art in question or, at the very least, to include cultural amateurs and specialists from other disciplines. Blind competitions would probably not work very well. Canada is such a small big country and its poets so well known to one another despite their burgeoning numbers and the fact that they tend to sound like lab-created language clones, that a jury would in many cases have little trouble recognizing an anonymous author from the style, subject and typical preoccupations of the submission. (I once tried the "blindfold" game myself and logged an over 60% success rate, though I have now begun training myself to forget rather than to retain such unprepossessing poetic "signatures"). Admittedly the game becomes somewhat more unmanageable as the numbers continue to explode but increasing familiarity with the work over time by those committed to the task inevitably reduces the chances of "error." The best that can be said of these poets is that they are equally boring but in different ways. So much for difference-in-identity. Still, reconfiguring the appraisal procedure would help turn a more or less predictable cakewalk into a genuine or at any rate more credible contest and encourage worthy writers who have given up on the Canada Council or approach it with trepidation to reapply with confidence in the fairness of its transactions. To support an emerging poet of promise or an established poet of talent within the limits of reasonable determination is a laudable aim, but one which patently requires a scrupulous and equitable jury process.

Mistakes will always be made but it is not reactionary of us to try to keep them from ramifying exponentially. Accordingly, a candidate should be judged not by one's so-called peers—who turn out more often than not to be either one's friends or enemies and sometimes one's former students or Creative Writing profs—but by the people one is ostensibly writing for. And if it happens that one is writing mainly for other poets, then one has no business applying for public or national largesse. Better the effusions of someone like Montreal street poet Hans Jacobs chalking his naïve and ephemeral lyrics on the pavements grey, for he at least engages directly with a lay audience and will never receive a grant. Or his local counterpart Michel Caïpèmdo who is refreshingly up front as a poetic capitalist;

currently selling his material at 25 cents per recitation, he dreams of opening a Web site to hawk his poems on the Internet. "If one person visited my site every second, just imagine how rich I'd be," he muses.

In any event, these are issues that must be dealt with before the situation is permitted to deteriorate any further. Since it is safe to assume that when it comes to the functioning of the poetry juries, motivation is often as suspect as intelligence, the dilemma has to be tackled head-on and sheltering organizations like the Canada Council made to sit up and take notice. For we are under no obligation to purchase the self-indulgent and insubstantial confections crowding the poetry market in this country. But neither should we be required to sustain a composite fiscal-and-aesthetic levy on our overtaxed resources to support a society of professional hangers-on, differentially adept at the merchandising of poetry but distressingly inept at the writing of it. How the soup gets made or the macaroni gets cooked is neither here nor there but how one gets on the gravy boat is a matter of no small importance.

Notes

1

If one wants to write a poem about onions and other roots and veggies stewing in a bouillon, one might look at Vivian Shipley's "The Difference Between a Raw Onion and a Slow-Cooked One" for pointers on how to go about it. The poem describes a pair of eldering lovers cooking together, layering the "flavors and textures" of a long relationship, relishing nostalgically how the cell walls of carrots and peppers are "firm as adolescent buttocks," observing how "baked garlic sags as it loses its fire,/but gains a touch of soul," and concluding:

> Generated by a convection oven, or by emotion,
> heat like passion changes everything, is able to
> melt solids to liquid, even within the human heart.

Now this is a poem that really cooks.

2

An illustration of our hectic distemper—the Dead Poets Walking syndrome—was provided at a poetry reading hosted by the Blue Metropolis literary festival in Montreal recently. Guest poets Robin Roberston (Scotland) and Thomas Lynch (U.S.) broke the general rule of chartered mediocrity, dazzling their audience with brief, commanding performances. But the Canadian contingent represented by nationally acclaimed poets Esta Spalding and Kate Braid read interminably to a rapidly increasing impression of cumulative embarrassment, revealing in the inert and uninflected nature of the material and the failure of knowing when to stop how far short they fell of the merit and tact exemplified by the invited readers. The effect was palpable and profoundly unsettling. Yet Spalding, Braid and their congeners are indefatigable participants in the national poetry scene, generating an extraordinary amount of buzz and promotional ferment. Could it be that they invest too much of their energy doing other things while at the same time remaining both prosodically oblivious and disablingly productive?

23

JOHN OF SALISBURY:
THE STATESMAN'S BOOK
AND ITS CONTEMPORARY
RELEVANCE

There are many theories purporting to explain the "march of history," as, for example, the hoary notion of "scientific socialism" with its dialectical certainties; the "great man" hypothesis that focuses on towering figures like Napoleon or Winston Churchill who determine the course of events; or the "from below" perspective treating of the lives and social movements of the lowly, marginal, oppressed or otherwise unacknowledged peoples, most famously espoused in Howard Zinn's politically skewed and tendentious *A People's History of the United States.*

One theory that receives little exposure we may call the idea of the "virtuous leader" as the indispensable factor that allows for the establishment of a decent, well-governed and "happy" state. The concept of the "virtuous leader" is a classical trope, going back to Epictetus (*Enchiridion*), Plato (*Republic*), Aristotle (*Nicomachean Ethics*) and Cicero (*On Obligations*). The idea enjoys little traffic because there are so few such leaders and because virtue itself is a problematic concept. Indeed, whatever "virtue" might entail, we are all, as poet W.H. Auden wrote, "articled to error." No human person, lay or elect, can be said to be unblemished, devoid of foibles, frailties and defects of character, but so unfortunate a fact does not invalidate the approach to an elusive standard of virtue and exemplary leadership.

The subject was taken up by John of Salisbury, a 12th Century theologian, philosopher and moralist who eventually became Bishop of Chartres and who is scarcely known today, but was an important figure in the late medieval Renaissance. An influential commenter on the affairs of the court of Louis VII, King of France (their dates are coterminous), with particular regard to Louis' wife, the celebrated Eleanor of Aquitaine, he understood courts and royal goings-on and was intimately acquainted with the consequences of troubled statesmanship. The *Policraticus*, translated as *The Stateman's Book*, is his most notable volume. As he writes, "This book concentrates in part on the frivolities of the courtiers . . . and busies itself with the footprints of philosophers" —a spectrum covering the terrain between foolishness and wisdom, the "yoke of vice" and the "rule of virtue."

The themes he addresses are perennially relevant and particularly so in our current historical moment. He deals with the corruption of court politics, the great good of free speech, and the need for a "virtuous ruler" who institutes just laws ensuring the liberty of the people. His strictures apply to the common individual as well; a state of virtue, he argues, cannot be attained without the exercise of personal liberty that permits what we would call today a "psychological space" for reflection and conscience. "He who is most virtuous," he writes, "is most free and the freest man enjoys the greatest virtue." The absence of freedom, both political and spiritual, guarantees intellectual debasement and moral degeneracy.

A just ruler is one who does not infringe on the private lives of his "subjects" —the concept of "citizen" had not developed in his time, but the implications are no less apposite today. The ruler must be "tolerant" of those he rules for "the necessity of tolerance gleams with a splendor all its own." Tolerance of a person's freedom to think for himself or herself, to arrive at rational conclusions, to believe in a higher power and serve a merciful God, to wish for harmony among peers, to preserve an independent spirit—such tolerance is a signal aspect of sovereign virtue, a gift of lawful charity from the ruler to the ruled.

At the same time, the desire to explore these exemptions from arbitrary domination—to think for oneself, to move freely in the public forum, to resist coercion and to refrain from abetting such coercion, i.e., to take advantage of what freedom has to offer rather than renounce or abuse it—constitute a material expression of personal virtue. One thinks of Hannah Arendt's remark from *On Liberty*, which applies to both ruler and subject, leader and citizen: "The raison d'être of politics is freedom, and its field of action is experience."

The idea of the virtuous leader has been much on my mind of late as I survey the lamentable spectacle of our national leaders across the West, particularly in light of COVID legislation and the swarm of idiotic and destructive mandates they have unleashed. I recall the essential distinction in the *Policraticus* between the "prince" and the "tyrant." The tyrant enslaves his people because he is himself enslaved to his ruling vice: unbridled ambition, the pursuit of limitless power, the levying of "mandates." His authority is thus illegitimate. The prince who governs properly understands that "authority cannot be recognized in violation of justice and the law"—whether the law of God, the law of Nature, or the law of the "purified conscience" and "instructed will"—for this is what John of Salisbury means by virtue as a prerequisite for enlightened leadership.

As always, there is a dearth of virtuous leaders, and the current crop is no exception; the vast majority are especially vain, shallow, hypocritical and dramatically unintelligent, as well as given to strongly leftist, dictatorial tendencies. There is little doubt what John would think of Barrack Obama, Joe Biden, Emmanuel Macron, Anthony Albanese, Justin Trudeau, Mark Carney, Jacinda Ardern, Keir Starmer and counting, not one of whom is remotely capable of even reading John of Salisbury, not one is even superficially familiar with the history of the Judeo-Christian West, not one, it seems, who has ever inspected his or her conscience, and not one who comprehends that political authority cannot cancel or override or willfully re-interpret long-standing provisions respecting rights and freedoms specified by a Constitution or a Charter. John would have made short work of them.

This is not to say that there is not a modicum of approximately "virtuous" leaders, as John might have realistically understood them. Their record may be checkered but they are not tyrants "who oppress a people by forceful domination." Hungarian prime minister Viktor Orban did impose the draconian COVID apparatus, but abolished Gender Studies in the universities, incentivized the family and population growth, and revived both the Hungarian spirit and economy. Former prime minister of Sweden Stefan Löfven, who stepped down in November 2021, helped to exacerbate the country's Islamic problem and aggressively promoted the wind farm boondoggle, yet wisely kept Sweden open during the pandemic. Donald Trump refused a salary and worked tirelessly to Make America Great Again, but blindly promoted Operation Warp Speed that deluged the country with problematic vaccines, opening the door to Big Pharma profiteering. I would consider these three, in the intermittent light of relative accomplishment, and making allowance for their evident flaws and misconceptions, as somewhat "virtuous" leaders. The jury is still out on Javier Milei of Argentina and Nayib Bukele of El Salvador, who (as of this writing) are new to the job, but they clearly have the makings of great leaders.

Clearly, John of Salisbury's conception of the "virtuous ruler" is a noble fiction, if not a political hallucination. Judging by overall results, however, we can say that there were—and are—good leaders, effective leaders, reasonably competent leaders, inspiring leaders, though few and far between. But the virtuous leader who aspires to moral perfection and profound insightfulness remains a shimmering mirage.

Was King David, beloved of God, defender of his nation, and ancestor of Christ, who lusted after Bathsheba and dispatched her husband to die in battle—was he a virtuous leader? In John's own epoch, were the ridiculous Louis VII and the treacherous Henry II caring shepherds of their flocks? Or the extraordinary Eleanor of Aquitaine, said to be the most beautiful and intelligent woman of her time— "this unusual woman in an age of virginal saints," as Thomas Cahill depicted her in *Mysteries of the Middle Ages*—married to Louis and then to Henry, and a sponsor of the failed and bloody Second Crusade, was she a virtuous leader? Has there ever been a King, Queen, president or ruler in all of human history fully approximating to the title? Perhaps the closest we may come to the archetype may be figures like the emperor Aurelius or Frederick the Great, but such are scarce. Nonetheless, the idea of the relation between justice, law, liberty and virtue summed up in the figure of the virtuous leader, as John of Salisbury described it, abides as a criterion of purpose, an ideal to be aimed at though never consummated.

As he wrote in a letter to an acquaintance, John knew that his book "would not likely find even one friend at court," and *The Statesman's Book* would surely find no readers and advocates in our current legislatures and parliaments. But it is far superior to all the manuals of diplomacy and remains a fresh reminder of the quest for decency and responsibility in the dispiriting turmoil of political maneuvering, an expression of the reign of the prince rather than the rule of the tyrant.

24
MYTH, REALITY,
AND ELECTRIC VEHICLES

Toadmeister, Sept. 26, 2024

Clearly, myth and reality are incompatible partners, especially when it comes to Electric Vehicles. A scalable model for a large consumer market is turning out to be a mirage. The market cannot sustain government-mandated folly and corporate fantasy, no more than the Soviet Union could sustain the Lysenko farce. Toxicity and undependability are the issues.

Lithium-ion batteries which power EVs represent a key technology that governments believe may enable mandated transitions to electric vehicles in many countries worldwide. But there remain several outstanding issues with lithium technology, including lifespan, cost and availability, battery performance at the extremes of ambient temperature, and the environmental impacts associated with the disposal of lithium battery components, whose toxic leakage can contaminate the soil and water table, as well as marine life. There is no such thing as the clean disposal of batteries.

Moreover, safety is major concern. Lithium battery electrolytes typically consist of 10 to 20 liters of an organic carbonate mixture containing ~1 Molar dissolved LiPF6 salt (lithium hexafluorophosphate, mainly used as lithium-ion battery electrolyte). Quantities of electrolyte will vary according to the EV model and the type of battery cell in use—cylindrical, pouch, prismatic—but the figure quoted is a standard approximation. Organic carbonates are flammable and present significant risks should they overheat in a process called thermal runaway. Moreover, LiPF6 is highly reactive to water; exposure to even low levels of humidity from the atmosphere leads to the formation of several chemical byproducts including hydrofluoric acid (HF), a residue produced when LiPF6 comes in contact with water or humidity.

Another major concern is safety. Lithium battery electrolytes typically consist of 10 to 20 liters of an organic carbonate mixture containing ~1 Molar dissolved LiPF6 salt (lithium hexafluorophosphate, mainly used as lithium-ion battery electrolyte). Quantities of electrolyte will vary according to the EV model and the type of battery cell in use—cylindrical, pouch, prismatic—but the figure quoted is a standard approximation. Organic carbonates are flammable and present significant risks should they overheat in a process called thermal runaway. Moreover, LiPF6 is highly reactive to water; exposure to even low levels of humidity from the atmosphere leads to the formation of several chemical byproducts including hydrofluoric acid (HF), a residue produced when LiPF6 comes in contact with water or humidity.

EVs suffer from an enormous number of additional problems that render their success extremely unlikely. These common deficiencies include not only limited travel range in the majority of EVs, long recharging periods and a paucity of recharging ports. We factor in as well high unit price, steep repair costs, extortionate insurance rates, fire department upgrades, prohibitive cost of battery replacement (upward of $20,000), negligible resale value, and damage to tires, roads, bridges, etc. due to excess weight. Add to this the punishing cost of running an EV, which *The Telegraph* calculates to be "twice as expensive as a petrol one," and we have every reason to shut the project down. The necessary rare earth metals, such as lithium, cobalt, graphite, nickel, and palladium, are labor-intensive, inherently noxious and exorbitantly expensive to extract.

Most of our political leaders, with the notable exception of Donald Trump, are absolute chumps and globalist hacks who have little knowledge of either economics, technology, or business. Profoundly superficial, they have not done their homework. Their thinking caps are obviously made in China of substandard materials and poor workmanship. Wedded to the counterfactual policies of a command economy, they refuse to back down as the Net Zero Fantasy runs headlong into reality and their nations lumber toward the precipice.

The January 2025 California wildfires proved many things—administrative incompetence, pervasive graft, DEI hiring disasters, and the abject stupidity of the common ruck of our leadership cadre—but also the hazardous unreliability of EVs, including those inevitable long line-ups at scarce charging stations, inordinate charge times, toppled power lines and electricity blackouts, and the poisonous properties of charred lithium hulks littering the area. Residents could not use their EVs to escape the devastation. At the same time, a fire broke out at the world's largest ion battery storage facility in Moss Landing, Monterey County, shutting down major sectors of the community and filling the air with toxic smoke. The fire re-ignited approximately a month later, forcing some residents to evacuate and others to be sealed inside their homes. The pristine Elkhorn Slough right by the facility, which feeds into the world-renowned marine sanctuary of Monterey Bay, was now testing with high levels of heavy metals.

The implications of the EV-battery issue recently came home to me with renewed force. Embarking on one of the myriad ferries that ply between Vancouver, the Sunshine Coast and the Gulf Islands,

I noticed a late-model EV among the hundreds of cars, trucks and tankers making the crossing. There were certainly more, but one was enough to get me worrying. A single "thermal event" would cause a near-unquenchable fire, release volumes of lethal emissions, and set off explosions in the confined hold of the ship that would likely result in its foundering and the death of many passengers from fire, poisonous fumes, and drowning.

I was encouraged to read that the Norwegian shipping firm *Havila Kystruten*, which operates car ferries around the coast of Norway, has banned the transportation of electric, hybrid and hydrogen vehicles. And with good reason. Neil Dalus of the freight insurer TT Club points out that "During a lithium battery thermal runaway event . . . significant amounts of vapour can be produced in many common supply chain scenarios, including ships' holds and warehouses."

Such calamities may not be as improbable as we may have thought. They are just waiting to happen. In 2022, the *Felicity Ace*, a large cargo vessel carrying 4000 cars, including EVs, not-so mysteriously caught fire and sunk. In July 2023, the Dutch vessel *Freemantle Highway* with a cargo of 3,783 vehicles, including 498 EVs, burst into flames, the fire starting "in the battery of an electric car," according to a crewman. EVs fitted with lithium batteries are ticking time bombs.

According to the president of the Global Automakers of Canada David Adams, billions in subsidies plus private investments "have set such large-scale projects in motion already, and this is part of the reason it's too late to turn back now . . . The die is cast." Adams, however, may be blowing smoke. Corporate receivership and national default are the more likely prospects. Myth and reality are incompatible partners. A scalable model for a large consumer market is turning out to be a mirage. The market cannot sustain government-mandated folly and corporate fantasy, no more than the Soviet Union could sustain the Lysenko farce. The collapse can't come too soon

25

DAYS OF WHINE
AND POSES: LITERARY
TYPES AND ACADEMIC
CONFERENCES

The garden flew round with the angel,
The angel flew round with the clouds,
And the clouds flew round and the clouds flew round
And the clouds flew round with the clouds

—Wallace Stevens, "The Pleasures of Merely Circulating"

On the eve of my departure for the New Writing Worlds Symposium at the University of East Anglia in Norwich, I received an email from a friend who had been a guest of the University some years before. "Beware," he cautioned, "you are entering a concrete prison from which you may never emerge." When I arrived the next day, I saw what had provoked his facetious warning. The heft and layout of the university buildings resembled a vast correctional facility, a complex of massive, louring, Bauhausian blocks scattered helter-skelter that had one promptly devising plans for escape. Its architect, Sir Denys Lasdun, had clearly transformed his Modernist dream of a communal living and working space into a scowling futurist nightmare straight out of Yevgeny Zamyatin's *We*, constructing, as the tale's protagonist says somewhere in the text, an impenetrable curtain that was about to cut him off from this whole beautiful world. I was reminded of Prince Charles' mordant comment on Lasdun's Royal National Theatre: "a clever way of building a nuclear power station in the middle of London without anyone objecting."

Interestingly, the University had become front page news as the home of the Hadley Climate Research Unit, now under a non-meteorological cloud for having contaminated much of the evidence promoting the theory of Anthropogenic Global Warming. I recall pausing before a strange, bartizan-like structure, a kind of Martello tower fused to an enormous ingot of glass and concrete, and wondering what purpose so bizarre an edifice might possibly serve. It was only in the last few months that I learned I'd been standing before the CRU building, described by Ian Wishart in *Air Con* as "one of the temples of global warming belief," sheltering a conclave of scientists whose analytic hijinks might have tempted one "to laugh out loud."

A couple of years down the road the shady characters inhabiting that antiseptic fortress would be outed as scientific frauds perpetuating a deception on a befuddled world, and its ringleader, Dr. Phil Jones, would be effectively compelled to resign. The CRU building, studded with tiny, machicolated windows from which to pour boiling oil and hurl rocks during a siege, seems an appropriate pile in the current circumstances. Although the university syndics, posing as an "International Panel," have just released a report attempting to rehabilitate the high priests of "climate change," I couldn't resist summing up the Hadley contretemps in an admittedly whimsical couplet:

The Lament of Phil Jones

We thought we were on to something, yet sadly
the world still goes on, but not the Hadley.

But more extenuating reports are sure to issue like projectiles from the Hadley oylets in the months ahead.

In any event, first impressions, even of Brutalist architecture, are notoriously unreliable. When the initial shock had worn off, I noticed that many of the petrified slabs that seemed to curtail one's sense of movement and latitude had begun to yield to the caressing ministrations of climbing ivy, the grim *lapidosus* gradually turning a rich, warm green as if nature abhorred a Lasdun and time could be counted on to succeed where man had failed. Had Malcolm Bradbury, co-founder of the creative writing department at East Anglia, written his *The History Man* today, with its description of "the local new university, a still expanding dream in white concrete, glass, and architectural free form," the edges of his satire might have softened with vegetal supplements and germinating borders.

Adding to my changing impression was the campus itself, spreading beyond the penal construct of stony confinement in Wordsworthian swards of rolling lawn and gentle slope and victory-signed with innumerable rabbits' ears. Indeed, I had never seen so many rabbits in my life, the consequence, I was told, of a biological experiment run amok. This laboratory miscarriage, I fancied, had changed a solemn professoriate into a warren of gamboling dons given their freedom at last. I suddenly felt as if I had stepped out of Le Corbusier's "machine for living" into *Watership Down.*

Then there was "The Broad," an icy, duck-dotted lake quarried out to the south of the campus where one could stroll and take the evening air after a strenuous day in the conference room and too many valedictory pints at the Union Bar. I was not especially surprised to learn that a number of carousing students had had their university careers cut short in its waters, tragic events which accentuated the paradox of university life and made me think as well in the course of my late walks of that sodality of writers whose trajectories had ended in disaster. Hopefully, some of those assembled at the round table would manage to circumvent such derelictions.

During the time I spent shuttling between my lodgings at Nelson Court and the conference sessions in the Council Chamber,

I was unable to shake this sense of contradiction, this feeling of internment mixed with intimations of deliverance. In this respect, the venue furnished a befitting frame if anomalous setting for the Symposium itself. On the one hand, there were the wide-ranging discussions on almost every aspect of literary endeavor, the occasional exhilarating insights of the participants, and the intellectual saunter into realms, if not always of gold, of literary viridian; and on the other, the intermittently oppressive repetition of self-evident themes, the obvious infatuation of some of the participants with the circumscribed self rather than the voluminous world, and the constraints of a politically correct and determined evasion of plain veracity and candor.

This dialectic of scope and bondage, of spontaneity and interdiction, rhyming the surrounding topography of oasis *cum* penitentiary, was both startling and predictable—startling because intellectual vision and inspiration are always arousing, and predictable because in any group of people, however erudite and accomplished, there is inevitably a hint, and sometimes more than a hint, of the lowest common denominator at work. The interplay of angel and cloud is ineluctable.

Thus, at the first night poetry reading, English poet George Szirtes respected the conventions of performance in delivering a series of beautifully crafted poems, some witty and flamboyant, others darkly meditative, but studiously avoiding those issues which a multicultural audience might find contentious or offensive. Palestinian poet Mourid Barghouti, on the other hand, sought to politicize the event by reading a long, problematic piece featuring his grandfather's rooted fist and the incursion of conscienceless bulldozers, indifferent to the fact that certain members of the audience might have a very different point of view from his and find themselves tempted to respond on a level alien to the proceedings. Szirtes was civil and impeccably courteous, aware of the gradients at work in symposia of this nature; Barghouti was consumed by an agenda and subject to his prejudices, reading propaganda rather than poetry.

Another of the conferees, Israeli novelist and Haifa University professor A.B. Yehoshua, no doubt taking a page out of John Gardner's *On Moral Fiction*, launched an impassioned address on the necessity for a reawakened moral fervor behind all literary commitment, dismissing the blandishments of theory, the frivolity of merely technical experimentation, and the fashionable preoccupation with the trivial and the mundane. He had no tolerance for the aesthetic brahmins who legislated against good stories, credible characters and healthy moral content in favor of partisan concerns or speculative attenuations. A murmur of discontent fibrillated through the room. The impact of his contestation might be controversial but it remains keenly illuminating and demands to be grappled with. His presence was enlivening and much appreciated.

In another session, Lancashire poet and well-known translator from the German, David Constantine, taking a page out of practically everyone else's book, argued for the particular virtue of literary language as truth-speak, dispelling the occlusions of corrupt description, political euphemism and hidden agendas. But in demonstrating how meretricious language mystifies what should be obvious, he cited a cluster of illustrations of a distinctly anti-American slant which undercut the purport of his message, forgetting that the choice of examples is no less important than the choice of words. This was mystification by the back door. While stressing that literary language should cast an intense light on the shadowy assumptions that words will often hide, his examples of disingenuous formulation, which positioned America as the self-interested aggressor in the war against Islamist terror, served to conceal a strong political bias, if not a deep-seated prejudice, associated with current academic thought and jargon—the ideological reflection of Bradbury's "pious modernismus and concrete mass." As David Lodge writes in *Home Truths*, another of his brilliant intellectual satires, "you falsify a conversation if you leave out any part of it."

After I took the floor to protest Constantine's casuistical prancing, asking him why he had not included citations from the numerous instances of Muslim doublespeak as well, if only to right the balance, Egyptian academic Leila Ahmed turned and sternly inquired, "What have you got against Islam?" The atmosphere grew decidedly frigid, as was to be expected in so PC a parietal climate when protocol is broken. This was obviously no place for an objection to what amounted to an implicit and widely shared *parti pris*, a groupthink brought about by a set of staple memes and cognitive bromides diffused through the prevailing pneuma. Few seemed to realize that Ms. Ahmed had just confirmed my point. I remembered Robert Hughes lamenting in *Culture of Complaint* that "the academy had gotten too fond of the tags and labels that substitute an easy moralism for thought and judgment."

For the rest of the day and evening I found myself *non grata*, the recipient of disapproving stares and cold shoulders, and briefly considered whether I should cut short my visit. "Tomorrow to fresh woods, and pastures new." Not that I was unduly upset, but I was nonetheless gratified when novelist Austin Clarke later approached me and, speaking for a small cadre of silent supporters, said, "You did good, man." And I felt particularly vindicated when I was rebuked in the TLS report on the symposium as an "awkward poet" who had put certain indecorous questions to David Constantine.

A compliment and an insult had the tandem effect, for myself at any rate, of retrospectively puncturing the sanctimonious tone of much of the proceedings. There is elation to be found even in the midst of the lugubrious, and some amusement, I confess, to bearding the lions of academic propriety. Even as one engages in the cut and thrust of the culture wars— "A friendless warfare!" to cite William Cullen Bryant's paean to intellectual battle, "lingering long/Through weary day and weary year" —one needs to retain a pinch of insouciance. Indeed, what Charles Sykes recommends in *A Nation of Victims* for the American university and American intellectual life in general applies across the board, and certainly across the pond: *"lighten up."*

Early one morning, as I went outside with my cigarette and coffee to think about the day's planned events, I noticed a gondola balloon sailing by overhead and was put immediately in mind of Yeats' ringing phrase, "Another emblem there!" Here was a great bag of hot air that aptly symbolized every literary and academic conference I have ever attended. At the same time, it is only fair to allow that without the fuel and medium of gaseous exhalations, the panorama unfolding beneath the observation basket would not have been available. Metaphorically speaking, the East Anglia Symposium was, for me, that high-wafting bladder, a combination of flatus and elevation, of vapour and loftiness. Indeed, the words "flatulence" and "afflatus" are etymologically related. It seems you can't have one without the other.

Later on, reflecting on this gathering of disparate minds, I concluded that despite my own contribution of dubious ventilations to the formal transactions—I stood by my informal and plainly objectionable outburst—I had also profited from the altitude afforded by the opportunity to speak and listen, to reflect upon subjects pertaining to my vocation, to agree and disagree, and to meet a number of extraordinary individuals who helped me broaden my views on the practice of literature. Among these excellent writers and professors whom it was both my pleasure and profit to have met, I would mention—apart from Szirtes, Clarke and Yehoshua—the American memoirist Eva Hofmann, the Danish novelist ib Michael and the expatriate Turkish fabulist Moris Farhi. One could only be grateful for participants like these, who added an element of both authenticity and levity to the laden academic noosphere.

As for most of the others, I regret to say that auditing their depositions was like plunging into "The Broad" or braving the fetid air of the Hadley building. Happily, there were one or two Morris Zapp types who would not have been out of place cavorting through the chapters of David Lodge's *Small World*, another enigmatic figure characterized by the earnest elusiveness of unintelligible babble who reminded me of Malcolm Bradbury's Doctor Bazlo Criminale, and even a rather barmy joker who seemed intent on emulating J.P. Donleavy's Sebastian Dangerfield in *The Ginger Man*, through without much luck.

Apart from these, the solid cohort of rote phalansterians was, naturally, *pro forma*, so assured in their ideological convictions and yet, as Hawthorne wrote of the socialist falanges in *The Blithedale Romance*, "so very faintly shadowed on the canvas of reality." And, of course, we had a couple of mandatory poets, aside from the ones I have mentioned, whose antics mirrored P.G. Wodehouse's Ralston McTodd in *Leave It to Psmith*, the author of *Songs of Squalor* featuring lines like "Across the pale parabola of joy." But at least an approximate balance between incompatibles could be maintained.

Nothing new here. One oscillates between the two extremes of ivy and concrete, of vigorous clarity and moral occultation, of cultivated discourse and rigid fustian, of good humor and bad cess— standard fare, I suppose, for all such belletristic colloquies. My friend was only partly right. The prison was also a greenhouse, and among the literary wardens intent on preserving ideological order, there were just enough gardeners to keep one believing in pastoral.

2 6

SCRAPPING GREEN

Wwwhat is wrong with Green? Plenty. To begin with, never credit anyone who wants to save the planet. Canada's prime minister wants to save the planet. Bill Gates wants to save the planet and relieve the plight of suffering humanity. Neo-Marxist Van Jones apparently experienced a divine revelation, enthusing in his book *The Green Collar Economy* that Green jobs will enable us to "heal the land and repair the soul." Al Gore, Leonardo DiCaprio, Cormac McCarthy, David Suzuki, James Hansen, John Kerry et al. want to save the earth. The list seems endless. Trust them at your peril. Citing *Climate Change Dispatch*, Catherine Salgado at *PJ Media* shows how "Climate alarmism is disastrous for the poor and middle classes, and benefits only the rich elites," who are exempt from the disadvantages of their own policies. "In other words, climate alarmism is a thoroughly Marxist and elitist movement."

Of course, not everyone is in it for profit. Filled to the brim with ideological conviction, eco-cultists bring to bear upon the empirical sphere of human life practices and attitudes that properly apply to the spiritual dimension. Far too many of these experts and activists are not so much dispassionate scientists or rational thinkers as they are pedestal theorists and instinctual religious crusaders, generally on the Left. Some mean what they say, having invested in an eschatological delusion; others are shrewd operators, having invested in power and lucre.

The numbers, graphs, charts and formulae regularly brandished before us to buttress the machinations of the eco-crowd look impressive, at least initially. Looks, as the old adage admonishes, can be deceiving, and this is doubly so when the partisans of an ominous intention cannily affect a passionate love for the planet and a solicitude for the future of humanity. For jostling among this zealous crew are some very cagey political practitioners who, in their peripatetic jog through the world media, have been hailed as bearers of the Olympic torch.

If one relies on observation and hard data rather than theory and agreeable factoids, it should be evident that the Green prepossession fails on almost every front. For example, Greens may worship the environment, writes Viv Forbes in *American Thinker*, "but support widespread environmental destruction by bird-chopping windmills, and land-stealing solar panels and their inevitable spider-webs of roads and transmission lines. All to produce intermittent energy that is forced onto distributers and consumers by legislated targets, taxes, subsidies and mandates."

Moreover, the enormous quantity of unassimilable toxic waste is never mentioned in the relevant literature. To take just one instance from a myriad. As *Townhall* observes (December 20, 2024) with regard to the Vineyard Wind project just off the Nantucket, Massachusetts coast, "Tiny razor-sharp shards of fiberglass, toxic fluids and chemicals, and various floating chunks from cooler to boat-sized fiberglass and styrofoam" from a shredded turbine blade have polluted the waters and beaches of the island. So predictable a disaster proves "that all the rosy promises from the wind developer were so much hooey."

Additionally, there is no word about the gargantuan amount of acreage required to support wind turbines. Author of *Bad Economics*

Peter Smith estimates that if wind were to supply 35 per cent of the world's electricity— "the lower end of the range desired by green activists—then about 1.2 million square kilometres would appear to be required," equivalent to eighteen times the land area of Tasmania or Switzerland or Virginia. Solar comes with its own issues—high maintenance, eventual disposability and toxic leakage.

By the same token, author of *Dumb Energy* Norman Rogers explains that solar is an economic disaster for utility companies as well as a deficit for customers living in regions without abundant sunlight who, unable to profit by "net metering" schemes, are forced to subsidize solar users in other parts of the country. Nor is there any word about the staggering amount of fossil-fuel energy necessary to create and back up panels and turbines or, as John Hinderaker shows in *Powerline*, little recognition of the fact that there is no feasible battery "that can store the entire output of a power plant or a wind farm" or successfully power ZEVs (Zero-Emission Vehicles). The requisite minerals, mainly nickel, cobalt and lithium, are rare, difficult to extract and insufficient to meet industry needs.

There are moral problems as well. We know that half of the world's supply of cobalt comes from the Democratic Republic of Congo, which uses child labor, that the necessary rare earth elements are almost entirely mined and refined in China, the world's greatest polluter, and that it takes 500,000 gallons of water to extract one ton of lithium, putting the lie to the ethical pretensions of the planet savers. As the scientific journal *Energy* reports, rare mineral extraction has severe impacts on health, "caus[ing] pollution and shortages of fresh water for local communities." These are all good reasons that putatively compassionate socialists and environmentalists— "So are they all, all honorable men," and, of course, women—should scrap the Green hornswoggle altogether. Claiming to give us a world powered by Green energy turns out to be nothing but a dirty trick. After all, there is, in the words of the *Energy* scientists, "no such thing as clean energy."

Finally, the Green prepossession is politically and economically ruinous, spelling the dissolution of advanced, free-market societies. Alexander Nussbaum has it pegged: "Global warming is a hoax, but not a standalone hoax. Memes band together for mutual survival. The global warming hoax is part of the 'progressive leftist' memeplex, together with other anti-American, anti-individual freedom, and anti–free enterprise dogmas." According to British economic historian Nicholas Crafts writing for *The Economic 2030 Inquiry* regarding the push for "net-zero," relying on British economic data over the period 1990-2008, decarbonization leads to steep economic decline.

Analogously, in *Green Tyranny: Exposing the Totalitarian Roots of the Climate Industrial Complex*, one of the most important books dismantling the climate scam, Rupert Darwall dissects "the role environmentalism would play" in the decay of capitalism into socialism, lavishly and ironically paying its way into accumulating debt, social breakdown and eventual totalitarian ascendancy. Intellectuals and academics with no understanding of industrial and economic reality become "anti-entrepreneurs," influencing business leaders and corporate interests who together pursue what political economist Joseph Schumpeter in *Capitalism, Socialism and Democracy* famously called "creative destruction." Except the destruction is hardly creative. The Green agenda calls for top-down control and central planning, establishing a managerial class "fuel[ing] . . . the engine of capitalism's self-destruction." Green begins as dark capital and ends as social bankruptcy.

How did we get to this impasse? As we have noted, amongst the Western public at large, as well as many of the "experts," global warming is more of a social, religious and political issue than a genuinely scientific one. German philosopher Peter Sloterdijk explains in *Terror from the Air* that we now live in an era of background "explication," preoccupied with "latency" and subject to the irruption of the invisible into our lives, culminating in an obsession with air.

(Today, of course, with aerosols.) As a result, "modern nation states and political media-commentaries" are fixated on a "historically new kind of conversation, best described as a 'climatological briefing'." Individuals are thus mustered into "an audience of connoisseurs under a common sky." From Sloterdijk's standpoint, we have become a community that, breathing "the ether of the collective," has succumbed to climatological madness and "will henceforth wage toxic war on itself." We re-inhale, he says, the "toxic communions" of our own "exhalate."

Ultimately, we are facing what economists call a "doom loop," which describes a situation in which one negative condition creates a second negative condition, which in turn creates a third negative condition or reinforces the first, resulting in a downward spiral. Columnist Spencer Fernando writing for the *National Citizens Coalition* may be right: "In many ways, the eco-radical movement resembles a death cult. It is obsessed with making the world 'pure,' focused on some kind of 'purifying' destruction to return humanity or the Earth to a more primitive state." In the last analysis, in order to save the Earth it is necessary to eliminate the human race, or at least reduce it to the status of its simian-like ancestors. As the old saying goes, save us from our saviors. The time has come to cool it.

27

ON GRAVITY

I have always been fascinated by gravity, mainly because I never understood it. Richard Feynman, who gave us the heuristic diagrams of quantum interactions, famously observed that "Nobody understands quantum mechanics"; the same is true of gravity. Like everyone, I know it as a tugging force, dragging you back as you climb a hill, pulling you forward as you descend—a force needing to be fought, to struggle against going up or coming down. Seeing images of astronauts floating in their space capsules was a reconciling factor; at least we were grounded, a relief not to find oneself in a condition of permanent levitation. Yet it remains a mystery defying resolution and comprehension.

It's common knowledge that gravity is one of the four fundamental forces of nature. The strong force binds the fundamental particles of matter together to form larger particles. The electromagnetic force consists of two parts, electricity and magnetism. The so-called weak force is responsible for particle decay, Schrödinger's Cat, and radioactivity, and has been descriptively combined with the former as the electroweak force—models predict it can be united with the strong force as the electronuclear force. Gravity is the feeblest of these forces, resisting unification with the other forces into a single equation.

Indeed, gravity remains one of the greatest problems for understanding the nature of the universe. Isaac Newton first proposed the idea of gravity as an attraction between two objects—the apocryphal apple—and developed, or discovered, the inverse square law to describe its operative principle. Albert Einstein in his theory of general relativity posited that gravity cannot be wholly or adequately described as an attractive force but is ultimately the effect of massive stellar objects bending space and time—a gravitational field minus gravity, so to speak, as it is generally felt and understood. Given an initial push in the Big Bang, for example, after billions of years planets would simply "follow the curve," banking hard like race cars in natural orbit around their stars or like supinated curveballs sinking toward the plate. What is called "gravitational lensing" is the effect of galaxies and clusters of galaxies, busy curving spacetime and bending light rays as they hurtle by.

But now we are given to understand that gravity is also a wave, a ripple in spacetime formed from the collision of massive stars and the merging of black holes—predicted by Einstein in 1916 and detected for the first time on September 14, 2015 at the Laser Interferometer Gravitational-Wave Observatory at the Hanford site in Washington State and dubbed, obviously, GW150914. As Govert Schilling explains in *Ripples in Spacetime*, gravitational waves are so extremely low-frequency—they can have, for example, a period of 30 years, which means a single wavelength is an almost ungraspable 30 light years—that it is something of a miracle they were ever detected. (Indeed, according to *Advanced Science News* (ASN), long-wave gravitational waves have wavelengths equivalent to around 110 million light-years, about the width of the Virgo Supercluster—a collection of galaxies that includes the Milky Way—with a frequency that is equivalent to the age of the Universe, around 13.8 billion years.) But the fact is: they exist. The evidence is clearly laid out in Kip Thorne's monumental *Black Holes & Time Warps*. (Thorne was an advising producer for the blockbuster film Interstellar. KIPP, one of the robots, is named after him.) As Brian Clegg explains in *Gravitational Waves*, these waves are contractions and expansions of the fabric of spacetime itself.

Bringing gravity into the family of forces in a single theoretical framework would then produce, according to the cosmologists, a Theory of Everything. So far gravity resists absorption. As Thorne wrote, "The gravitational universe [looks] extremely different from the electromagnetic universe." Hence, the problem for a layman like me. I simply cannot see how gravity can be simultaneously an attractive force, a curvature in spacetime, and a nanohertz wave propagating at the speed of light. When I trudge up a hill, do I feel an adhesive force emanating from the earth beneath my feet, grappling at my ankles and causing me to labor upward, or is spacetime bending under and around me, so that I'm really just orbiting, or is a mysterious wave from the remote corners of an expanding universe somehow applying a ghostly velcro to my heels? When I let my pen drop a quarter inch to the tabletop, does it fall because a force is pulling it down, because the quarter inch of space has looped inward owing to the mass of the table, or because two black holes slammed into one another 1.3 billion light years distant, like the GW150914 discovered at Hanford and now cresting around my pen, or is an effect of something called quantum gravity caused by a massive black hole collapsing the framework of spacetime?

There are other complicating issues warping around the gravity riddle. Quantum mechanics, string theory and the postulate of multiple universes introduce hypothetical explanations for the existence and effects of this enigmatic force. Perhaps quantum particles called gravitons exert a furtive impact on the macroworld—but no one can understand what quantum gravity does at 10-xx second intervals. As Carlo Rovelli writes in *The Order of Time*, "That the gravitational field has quantum properties is a shared conviction, albeit one currently supported only by theoretical arguments rather than by experimental evidence." Indeed, the argument that quantum fields might interact with spacetime curvature to explain how gravitational effects might emerge from quantum field interactions leaves me floating helplessly like a mentonaut in some cortical capsule, a Major Tom lost in the vacancy of space.

Perhaps, according to string theory, our universe is a brane or a sheet of spacetime hanging out in a higher dimensional space in close contact with other branes that leak across, producing what we know as gravity. Perhaps gravity is "weak" only in a 3-dimensional world; add a few extra dimensions and presto! gravity flexes its muscles, like the skinny guy in the old Charles Atlas commercial. Perhaps, a parallel universe—according to Richard Panek's *The Trouble with Gravity*, merely one of potentially 10-500 such universes— generates perturbations in our home universe, which we recognize as gravity.

As Panek writes, "gravity might be something that bleeds into our universe from an adjoining universe, or it's an artifact from a colliding universe"—which may explain why physicists cannot understand or unify gravity in a single equation with the other three forces of nature. In any event, I find it hard to imagine that universe X has cut a dimensional incision between pen and tabletop such that the pen has nowhere to go but in a direction that we know as "down." Or are we observing the parallax nature between local flatness and global curvature, between tiny intervals of space and time stitched together like little fishnet parallelograms or metrical coefficients to construct a large, curved global structure. Engineer and science writer John Stoddard in *Relativity Theory* calls it "mapping the potato." The coordinate system is covariant in any number of dimensions, which doesn't help me much.

And so, the layman scratches his head and wonders. Discounting gravitons, branes and parallel universes, which remain unintelligible or, as Neil Turok pronounces in *From Quantum to Cosmos: The Universe Within*, "empty model universes" that cannot be used "to describe expanding universes full of matter and radiation like ours," the question persists: Is what we call gravity actually three distinct phenomena—attractive force, curvature of space, pulses of waves—operating at different levels, intervals and regions in the universe?

Or should we seriously countenance the quantum hypothesis as a fourth possibility, a force-bearing particle, or graviton, that mediates gravitational interactions at infinitely small scales in the form of discrete, tiny, pixel-like chunks, known as quanta? Are we witnessing the effects of the entanglement between the quantum particles of spacetime, manifesting as a kind of "emergent gravity" or "entropic force," as Dutch theoretical physicist Erik Verlinde has postulated? (Shan Gao in *Understanding Gravity* thinks Verlinde may be a successor to Newton and Einstein.) The theory of quantum gravity attempts to reconcile the structure of physical reality on very small scales (quantum mechanics) and very large scales (gravity as experienced), but the trouble is that the search for a force-bearing particle, or graviton, has not yet borne fruit. Again, as Carlo Rovelli writes in *The Order of Time*, "There is not yet a theory of quantum gravity that has been generally accepted by the scientific community." We're still stuck.

Or is gravity simply one inscrutable power that is somehow diffracted, as through a prism, into four observable franchises advertised in four different formulaic ways? Some time ago, I ordered via Amazon's various buying options a rare book by theoretical physicist John Wheeler, which I was told by an equally baffled physicist friend might help me make some sense of the question. Though

I ordered the book from several different outlets, it never arrived. Perhaps it was sucked into a black hole.

Here I should add an explanatory remark to the reader. Though in my daily work I continue to focus on poetry, literary criticism, politics and social commentary, I am convinced that absolute truth—or at least stable truths—can be found only in the scientific realm, in chemistry, physics and math, founded on fundamental principles of observation, testable theory, experimental confirmation and Karl Popper's notion of falsifiability, articulated in his *The Logic of Scientific Theory*. For a theory to be accepted as scientific, it must be capable of being subject to proofs of falsifiability. The problem with the discursive fields of commentary, scholarship, the misnamed "social sciences" (which are not sciences and seem to be becoming increasingly anti-social), and the Humanities in general (with the exception of music, which is built on mathematical ratios) is the inevitability of bias, prior convictions and assumptions, and partisan viewpoints that can never be ruled out.

Expository writers—at any rate, the good ones—are also searching for truth, but in the human sphere of culture, politics, society and history. Here the quest for truth is shadowed by the intrusion of personal values and beliefs whose moral component is never rigorously assured. Quarrels and contestations are part of the game. There are strongly held personal convictions and considerable bickering in science, too, but eventually incontestable fact, if not absolutely unsettled truth, will emerge. 2 plus 2 will always equal 4—but poet e.e. cummings can plausibly title a volume *Is 5*.

The distinction between the two spheres of investigation is commonly construed as the difference between subjective parallax and objective methodology. Good poetry will usually deal with issues of considerable gravity, as it were, but felt truth is not the same as analytic or deductive truth. We might say that we are dealing with a homespun version of the "gravity anomaly," the difference, as William Lowrie points out in his *Fundamentals of Geophysics*, between the observed value of a gravitational reading and the theoretical or predicted value, in which the latter does not necessarily conform to the practical measurable datum.

Even if ultimate truth continues asymptotically to recede, even if science is never settled, which is as it should be, the quest for reliable knowledge is authentic, impartial, scrupulous, never-ending and honorable, producing disparate but incontrovertible results in various fields of inquiry that can test true, as evidenced by practical applications. That's why your GPS works. That's why almost every appliance you take for granted works. Such facts, or designated truths, account for the basic morality of scientific inquiry, its "ethical importance," as Erwin Schrödinger writes in *My View of the World*, and which he regards as no less compelling than its "logical force."

It is impossible to lie in science, that is, in real science as opposed to politicized science™, which is all the rage among the profoundly superficial speculators who throng the profession at present. Errors will be made, but they are correctible. Science practiced honorably and moving toward objective conclusions is as close as we can get to truth, which exerts its own species of intellectual and spiritual gravity. That is why, perhaps, science is as close as we can get to God. As for the truth of gravity itself, admittedly, it continues to escape me, as it does my betters. Perhaps one day Wheeler's book will arrive.

28

BALLS AND STRIKES: THE ISRAELI DILEMMA

We can all too easily look back on scenes of unthinkable horror perpetrated by those who would do anything rather than give the Jews their due.

—Thomas Cahill, *The Gifts of the Jews*

In *How to Do things with Words*, philosopher J.L. Austin makes a useful distinction between two kinds of speech acts, the referential and the constative. The referential delineates an actual state of affairs, the constative establishes not a quality but a social function. Austin offers an analogy from baseball: the ball may travel knee-high across the center of the plate, a perfect strike, but if the umpire calls "ball," that's how it registers on the scoreboard and operates in the game.

For much of the world today, that is, for "umpires" engaged in the production of figments and bent on the reconstruction of reality, an Israeli "strike" will almost always count as a "ball." The referential has been reconfigured as the constative, despite what a later replay may bring to light. Thus, the Israeli pitcher throws strikes; the Arab batter receives a base on balls. An intimate congruence has been performatively created between the report and the referent minus the slightest hint of the semantic distance that stretches between the two. The former remains parasitic upon the latter.

Archeologist and historian David Meir-Levy makes this clear in his important book with its Austinesque title, *History Upside Down: The Roots of Palestinian Fascism and the Myth of Israeli Aggression,* in which he digs up the buried facts and returns to the referential. He points out that "the Arabs of the area in question had their own designation for the contested region: Bilad al-Sham" (the country, or province, of Syria/Damascus/Levant.) In point of fact, according to census records, approximately half the Arab residents of the area under contention arrived as settlers from south-Syria after the breakup of the Ottoman empire. It appears they might plausibly constitute the real "occupation."

It was only after the 1967 war that the Palestinian Liberation Organization (PLO) reframed the issue, Meir-Levy writes, by "inventing a 'historic Palestine' ex nihilo, an ancient 'Palestinian people' who had lived in their 'homeland' from 'time immemorial' [and] who were forced from their homeland by the Zionists . . . " Similarly, in her indispensable volume *Islam and Dhimmitude,* celebrated Middle East scholar Bat Ye'or makes mincemeat of the Palestinian brief; they are "an invented people, devoid of national particularisms and history, and artificially constructed . . . They are not a 'Palestinian people' but Arab refugees." Her research is impeccable and naysayers cannot fault it without befouling themselves. Indeed. the idea of a (constative) Palestinian nation was hatched principally by Yasser Arafat, who did not disguise his genocidal intentions. In his own words, the aim of the PLO was "not to impose our will on [Israel], but to destroy it in order to take its place." (*Fact Real,* December 13, 2011)

In the current imbroglio, as always, the loaded term "occupation" is used as a weapon against Israel when the bald facts are that Gaza is an autarchical quasi-state; the "West Bank" presently controls 94% of the territory it sits on, with Israel retaining a defensive buffer zone; and in the Palestinian lexicon the term "occupation" alludes to the whole of Israel. Unfortunately, the Israeli state of mind, once the country's defensive needs are more or less served, has been until recently largely concessionary, whereas the Palestinian mentality is largely rejectionist. As anthropologist Philip Salzman points out, the Palestinians do not want a two-state solution; "they want one state from the river to the sea." (*PJ Media*, March 26, 2024.)

However, when in 1994 Israel and Jordan signed a peace agreement, Jordanian control of the "West Bank" was officially relinquished to Israel and not to the Palestinian Authority. Again, from the legal, as well as practical, perspective, there is no Israeli "occupation," as (mis)understood by the political echelon, the press and a profoundly misinformed public. This is one of the greatest canards to issue from the conflict. Once again, a "strike" has been interpreted as a "ball" and a foul ball has morphed into a home run. This is the essential point. How easily a glaring constative is transformed into a counterfeit referential.

All this reminds me of a game of chess I once played in a Casablanca hotel with an Egyptian fellow-guest. I soon found that none of the accepted moves applied—rooks moved anywhere they pleased, knights were permitted two hops, bishops slid laterally as well as diagonally, pawns could capture and then return to their original squares. The structure of the game was made up as we went along. When I protested, I was condescendingly informed: "That's Egyptian chess."

When it comes to Israel, the constative will almost always euchre the referential and a collective assessment obliterate a singular factor. Whether improvised on the spot or of long duration, apocryphal rules are like counterfeit currency, bad ideas driving out good and leading eventually to anarchy. Egyptian chess or baseless ball are dead ends. In any event, the fix is in and the game is rigged.

To revert to Austin's metaphor, if Israel had the best baseball team in the world, it would still lose the publicity game to a bunch of Arab sad sacks by a lopsided score. The principle of playing by the rules has taken on an entirely different meaning. The rules are meant to distort rather than reflect the real or order the welter of experience, a way of lying that approximates the nimbus of truth. That's the "beauty" of it. After all, it's official. It's just not true.

Austin would have been appalled by the casual and uninformed, if not downright malevolent, conflation of the two formulaic realms, the factitious constative and the factual referential. And so should we all.

29

THE FAKE COMPASSION
OF THE LEFT

Their masters did not love them, and planned to replace
them with other peoples.

—Renaud Camus, *Ørop*

The verses of the medieval Persian poet Saadi Shirazi, *Bani Adam*, or "Children of Adam," are sewn into a carpet with golden thread and prominently displayed at the UN headquarters in New York. A gift from the Islamic Republic of Iran in 2005 in a gesture of ineffable irony, the poem's sentiment of unity and compassion between all human beings was meant to convey the ostensible spirit of the United Nations' Universal Declaration of Human Rights, the concept of the Dialogue among Civilizations, and the quest for a borderless world. A loose translation of the verses reads:

Bani Adam

All of the sons of Adam are part of one single body
They are of the same essence.
When time afflicts us with pain
In one part of the body
All the other parts feel it too.
If you fail to feel the pain of others
You do not deserve the name of man.

The poem has been interpreted by delegates at the UN and apparatchiks in many governments to justify the acceptance of illegal migrants by the hundreds of thousands or millions, in addition to the legal importation of multitudes from Third World countries. The citizens of Europe and North America have been told repeatedly, directly or indirectly, that they must not refuse those afflicted "with pain." If they fail to heed "the pain of others," they are fascists, far-right, inhuman.

This interpretation has ignored the pain of those who have seen their own countries transformed by mass migration, which has increased crime, social division, fear, and economic immiseration. Their pain, in seeing the ways and usages of their country disrespected and destroyed, does not register with those who profess such love for the "children of Adam."

These verses may also be challenged and adapted by conservative thinkers and politicians to defend their own citizens from the destructive and conquering effect of interlopers from abroad exploiting the resources—economic, educational, medical and cultural—of the host nations.

In fact, the solicitude for others affected by the majority of UN delegates and state actors is plainly counterfeit, a deceptive expression of ulterior motives involving calculations of profit, surreptitious political agendas, the inflaming of ancestral hatreds, the pursuit of global hegemony, and other invidious purposes and programs such as those venerable canards climate change, pandemic preparedness and open borders.

Regarding the latter, French political philosopher Renaud Camus has charted the "great replacement" of European peoples by Third World migrants and immigrants in "our mad embrace of a posthuman future." Camus has been dismissed as representative of the so-called "fascist right," but the truth is that he is a conservative scholar deeply concerned with the imminent dissolution of the Judeo-Christian West and the death of his beloved Europe. In his attempting to beat back the replacement movement, one may consider him as the intellectual Charles Martel of our era, the Christian warrior who repelled an army of Muslim invaders at the Battle of Tours in 732. One thinks, too, of the 1683 Siege of Vienna, broken by a combined force led by Polish king Jan Sobieski.

For Camus, the old adage that charity begins at home is as magisterial a truth as one could hope to find. This opens a second, equally crucial matter: what is home? To begin with, home is family, one's forebears and descendants, one's culture and history, one's defenders and dependents, those who have labored to establish a moral conception of the good and a shared tradition of common life and mutual responsibility. Home is where rules of conduct and norms of usage are implicitly in force and a spirit of intimacy forms an ideal bond between members of a community of variable dimensions. As Robert Frost writes in *Death of the Hired Man*, "Home is the place where, when you have to go there,/They have to take you in." Home is where people know what to expect of one another, a line that traces the boundary between the familiar and the alien.

In other words, *home is a function of recognized borders*. When the sense of home and all that it implies of security and reciprocity has been put "in place," one can then turn one's attention outward to humanity as a whole, to feel empathy for the stranger, and to transact with the world outside one's borders, especially when it becomes necessary to protect the home itself. Of course, one can think of the planet as a home for which we are all responsible, but such responsibility is often misplaced, an ideological indulgence, and can lead to the ruination of the more embordered home we live in. We fight the canard of "climate change" at the expense of domestic prosperity and even national survival.

At this point a brief digression may be in order regarding the poem itself, as expressing a sentiment that is at least partly false and surely illogical. A pain in the finger does not register as a hurt in the knee. The parts of the human body, like the body of nations, are both connected *and distinct*. Moreover, the parts of the body are not equal in terms of their capacity for pain or their importance to the whole. One may lose a toe or a limb and still survive. One cannot lose a vital organ like the heart or the pancreas and continue to live. There is a hierarchy of indispensability, which Shirazi has smothered in an access of sentimentality. The concluding two lines are uplifting and possibly true, but the operative analogy is flawed.

Equality of personal or existential value only makes sense with reference to the *optimal impartiality* of the law, which treats both the beggar and the king, the toe and the heart, as equal before the tribunal of justice, as stipulated by the Magna Carta. Within the democratic community, all the parties are meant to be weighed as equal, not in the crucial importance of their particular functions, but in their legal status as citizens. However, this is not what Shirazi is getting at and is certainly not the ethos at work in Iran or in failing nations that have ceased to believe and participate in a set of common standards beneficial to all, maxims predicated on a plinth of shared moral principles and judicial evenhandedness.

Bani Adam is a beautiful idea, but it is completely mistaken and beguiling at its metaphorical core. Both dedicated globalists and patriotic nationalists, despite their inability to critique the poem validly, read it in antithetical ways. Two important historical figures have articulated these differing conceptions of the family of mankind.

Dean of St. Paul's Cathedral and metaphysical poet John Donne (1572-1631) famously wrote in his *17th Devotion*, "No man is an island, entire of itself; every man is a piece of the continent, a part of the main. If a clod be washed away by the sea, Europe is the less, as well as if a promontory were . . . any man's death diminishes me, because I am involved in mankind, and therefore never send to know for whom the bell tolls; it tolls for thee." The purport of Donne's sublime words is identical, at any rate on the surface, to the exalted sentiment of Shirazi's verses, but the problem remains. One cannot belong to others if one does not belong to oneself, as

Confucius wisely acknowledged in his *Analects*: "To put the world in order, we must first put the nation in order; to put the nation in order, we must first put the family in order; to put the family in order; we must first cultivate our personal life; we must first set our hearts right."

In a FoxNews interview (January 31, 2025), American vice president J.D. Vance put the matter succinctly: "There is something very deranged in the mind of the far left in this country, where I really do think they feel more of a sense of compassion for illegal aliens who have no right to be in this country than they do for their fellow citizens. As an American leader, but also just as an American citizen, your compassion belongs first to your fellow citizens."

In the Hebrew bible the hierarchy of obligations, knows as *Tzedaka*, begins with one's family and people, before spreading outward, as in *Deuteronomy* 15:7: *Thou shalt open thine hand wide unto thy brother, to thy poor, and to thy needy, in thy land.* The medieval Jewish sage Maimonides in his halakhic compendium the *Mishneh Torah* distinguishes eight levels of charity the greatest of which is to support one's co-religionists. Christianity—Judaism's only begotten son—elaborates the same notion through scripture and philosophy. St. Thomas Aquinas teaches the *ordo caritatis*, the order of charity, in his *Summa Theologiae* (II, II, Question 26): "in matters pertaining to nature we should love our kindred most, in matters concerning relations between citizens, we should prefer our fellow-citizens, and on the battlefield our fellow-soldiers." According to Catholic doctrine, writes C.S. Lewis in *The Abolition of Man*, "we must love things to the degree they ought to be loved." Canon lawyer Father Gerald Murray, quoted in *LifeSite* (January 29, 2025), refers to the Church teaching that "a state has the right to and obligation to regulate the life of society." The principle is effectively universal.

These issues have become critically pertinent today as foreign bodies like the UN and its allies, the World Economic Forum (WEF) and the World Health Organization (WHO), along with the ruck of progressivist politicians, plot to assume autocratic control of the public policies of Western nations. They rely on Shirazi's poem—or what amounts to the same thing, the "social justice" humbug—as cover for their nefarious intentions.

The conservative position is that the president or prime minister of any country should be primarily concerned with the people of his own nation, aiming to achieve both economic growth and individual liberties. Compassion and benevolence should not be outsourced to foreign agencies who affect to act on our behalf, or deposited as desiderata in the portfolios of leaders whose interests lie elsewhere than with their own constituents.

Political leaders of integrity who understand that responsibility is local before it is universal are the true exponents of compassion. They are those who wish to preserve the freedom and security promised by constitutional government, who are faithful to their people, who feel the pain of others whom they have sworn to serve, and who, in the last analysis, deserve the name of man.